ANCIENT EGYPTIAN PHARAOHS

ANCIENT EGYPTIAN PHARAOHS

JO FORTY

This edition published 1998 by
PRC Publishing Ltd,
Kiln House, 210 New Kings Road
London SW6 4NZ

Published in the USA by JG Press, 1998
Distributed by World Publications, Inc.,
455 Somerset Avenue, North Dighton, MA
02764

ISBN 1 57215 253 2

Printed in China

Title Page: Impassively beautiful, a colossal statue of Ramesses II — an idealized portrait of total power and majesty.

Right: An obelisk from Karnak. Originating at Heliopolis, obelisks represent the sun's rays as well as the ancient *benben* stone, symbol of the mound of creation.

Overleaf: Wall painting from the tomb of Tutankhamun, showing him between Hathor, Goddess of the West, and the jackal-headed Anubis, a God of the Dead closely associated with embalming and mummification.

CONTENTS

MONARCHS OF THE NILE

The Ancient Egyptian pharaohs were god-kings, worshipped as divine beings who were a living manifestation of the bridge between humanity and the gods. Maintaining the equilibrium of the universe through a mixture of policy and ritual, magic and might, fear and beneficence, their collective contribution built one of humanity's earliest and longest-lasting socio-political structures — a civilization spanning well over three millennia.

The pyramids built by the pharaohs — places of ascension linking them to the cosmos and the Afterlife — were the largest stone buildings in the world until the nineteenth century. The fabled riches of the pharaohs put more recent monarchies in the shade; their religious codes rival any in their complexity; and their art and sculpture reveal an advanced and aware culture that reaches out across time to touch us with wonder, and put our own civilization into perspective.

These achievements are even more astonishing when one considers they were brought about by an agriculturally-based Bronze Age society lacking any great technological base.

Ancient Egypt is in exactly the same place as modern contemporary Egypt, only for the most part (as in all older civilizations) underneath. Only about five percent of the country is inhabited, the rest is largely empty desert. That five percent of vital fertile land is the "gift" of the great river that flows all the way out of the central African highlands to the Mediterranean — the Nile. This water road became the thread that linked the Two Lands and its constancy enabled a civilization to evolve that would be the leading edge of man's development for a thousand years.

Within Egypt itself the Nile has two distinct parts: in the south, it is bordered by a slim band of cultivation by the river's edge, at its thickest only a few kilometers wide; in the north, there's a huge, fertile, fan-shaped delta, as the river breaks up into various tributaries before reaching the sea. These two distinct parts were the "Two Lands" of ancient times, the domain of the pharaohs. Even now in the modern state, Egyptians notice the differences between the desert and the delta in the character of their own population, as it was in ancient times. The "Two Lands" were held together only by strong pharaohs who could prevent the natural inclination of geography and nature to let them go their separate ways. Upon this contradiction Ancient Egypt was founded and, later, foundered.

A narrow strip of lush green fields and palm trees, surrounded on each side by dry dusty desert, is given life by the great River Nile flowing through their midst. The annual inundation is relied upon to nourish and refresh the soil; if it fails once, crops are thin and poor. If it fails for two years running, famine sets in — the flood is that critical to life along the Nile.

The Beginning

In the beginning — in pre-dynastic times some 5,000 years ago — Neolithic hunter-gatherers settled along the Nile's edge as the Sahara dried out, gradually co-operating more and more in the management of the annual inundation that occurred with a convenient and dependable regularity. This flood brought with it a rich, black, alluvial silt to fertilize their fields. On this crucial factor all else was built: so fundamental was the river cycle to their way of life, that the three seasons of the ancient calendar were named

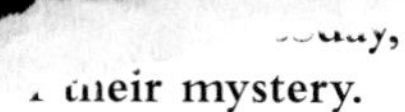

..uy,
. their mystery.

Akhet (inundation), *Peret* (growth), and *Shemu* (drought). The agriculture that developed with the aid of the river was the main occupation of the population, who from independent beginnings organized themselves progressively into villages, towns, cities, federations of communities, and then provinces — the later "nomes." These evolved through the gradual collective discovery of strength through unity, without which agriculture and river defense would be impossible.

The increase in the domestication of animals and the development of crops and irrigation led to a concomitant rise in the level of organization, order, and heirachy. The need arose for a strong ruler to control the people in the management of the river's annual flood, as well as to defend the territory. As the importance of the leader grew, so this brought the development of royalty, with its insignia and protocol.

During this period the foundations of the later state were laid. In fact, as far back as the pre-dynastic Naqada I and II (or Amratian/Gerzean) periods, the essentials were already coming into existence — the heraldic significance of Horus as an image of kingship, the commemorative "smiting icon" of victory, a prototype hieroglyphic language in the process of development, palettes for eye paint and more. Life depended on fertility and this was encouraged through the use of magic and the correct worship of the gods. With the naming of things power could be exhorted or given over them. This concept was to have great significance and application in the future culture.

It seems probable that the art of making bronze was introduced to the lands of Egypt from Mesopotamia; certainly there were some initial influences from Asia, perhaps an incursion by technologically copper-advanced adventurers, but there was no wholesale conquest, more of an absorption.

Religious development came directly from the environment. It was based on the sun and the river — the essential providers of life: Horus, the warrior hawk, the highest living creature who came out of Re, the sun, and was therefore manifested in him, and Osiris — initially the earth god of fertility, who rescued men from ignorance and savagery — by showing them how to grow food and domesticate beasts. There were a myriad other gods belonging to each locality; the desert and the river animals were all represented and combined with humans, too, in a dual form of representation.

Between the time of Narmer and Djoser everything that Egypt later became was already intrinsically in place, poised to explode into a reality that would lead to the Old Kingdom and the magnificent great pyramids. It was a time of experimentation and confidence. The archaeological remains available to us initially color our view: their funerary and mortuary spheres are the only real hard evidence; much else is hidden by time, though there are clues to their ways of life. It is all too easy to think

The only survivor in the modern age of the Seven Wonders of the Ancient World, the Giza pyramids of Khufu and Khafra are seen from across the river. Despite their age and condition, they are still hugely impressive today, and have lost little of their mystery.

Akhet (inundation), *Peret* (growth), and *Shemu* (drought). The agriculture that developed with the aid of the river was the main occupation of the population, who from independent beginnings organized themselves progressively into villages, towns, cities, federations of communities, and then provinces — the later "nomes." These evolved through the gradual collective discovery of strength through unity, without which agriculture and river defense would be impossible.

The increase in the domestication of animals and the development of crops and irrigation led to a concomitant rise in the level of organization, order, and heirachy. The need arose for a strong ruler to control the people in the management of the river's annual flood, as well as to defend the territory. As the importance of the leader grew, so this brought the development of royalty, with its insignia and protocol.

During this period the foundations of the later state were laid. In fact, as far back as the pre-dynastic Naqada I and II (or Amratian/Gerzean) periods, the essentials were already coming into existence — the heraldic significance of Horus as an image of kingship, the commemorative "smiting icon" of victory, a prototype hieroglyphic language in the process of development, palettes for eye paint and more. Life depended on fertility and this was encouraged through the use of magic and the correct worship of the gods. With the naming of things power could be exhorted or given over them. This concept was to have great significance and application in the future culture.

It seems probable that the art of making bronze was introduced to the lands of Egypt from Mesopotamia; certainly there were some initial influences from Asia, perhaps an incursion by technologically copper-advanced adventurers, but there was no wholesale conquest, more of an absorption.

Religious development came directly from the environment. It was based on the sun and the river — the essential providers of life: Horus, the warrior hawk, the highest living creature who came out of Re, the sun, and was therefore manifested in him, and Osiris — initially the earth god of fertility, who rescued men from ignorance and savagery — by showing them how to grow food and domesticate beasts. There were a myriad other gods belonging to each locality; the desert and the river animals were all represented and combined with humans, too, in a dual form of representation.

Between the time of Narmer and Djoser everything that Egypt later became was already intrinsically in place, poised to explode into a reality that would lead to the Old Kingdom and the magnificent great pyramids. It was a time of experimentation and confidence. The archaeological remains available to us initially color our view: their funerary and mortuary spheres are the only real hard evidence; much else is hidden by time, though there are clues to their ways of life. It is all too easy to think

Left: Majestic Horus, the symbol of the royalty and power of the pharaohs throughout Ancient Egyptian history. This statue is in the Temple of Horus at Edfu.

Right: The Giza necropolis at night. A *son et lumière* lights up the pyramid of Khafra with the Sphinx in the foreground. Khafra's pyramid still possesses a small amount of the original white limestone with which it was faced, capping the apex like snow on a mountain top.

of the Ancient Egyptians as gloomy and death-obsessed, because most of what remains of them today is to do with death. This is not really the case. In fact, their lifestyle was so pleasant and easy that the Egyptians conceived of heaven and earth as being one and the same place. They were keen for it never to end, and pursued a natural progression from the intense love of life to a wish to continue it.

The pyramids and their accompanying mortuary complexes should be seen as buildings similar in significance to the cathedrals of the Middle Ages. They represent a communal effort and focus, a kind of spiritual power station for the maintenance of the order of the universe. Only later, when they had failed to guard the tombs of their kings, but rather advertised their presence, did they change to hidden syringe and tunnel tombs, complete with false steps and elaborate camouflage. The Egyptian people, from time immemorial, were always a cosmopolitan race, even the highest in the land — the pharaohs themselves, as their names testify — were from a wide racial base. Over time different peoples were absorbed into the native population: African, Berber, Bedouin, Semitic, Greek, and Levantine.

The actual tools of everyday Egyptian life were ephemeral, made from woods, reeds, rushes, and mud-brick. For Egyptians it was only eternity that needed a more solid construction: they believed that the soul dwelt in heaven and the body on earth. Rejecting the idea of reincarnation, they saw the underworld and life as two distinct parts of the same intrinsic reality — hence the similarity of requirements on either side, boiling down to a living form and a spiritual form, requiring symmetry and balance. The personality resided in the body, while the *Ka* —its spirit double — continued in the corpse. This process took time and protocol to happen; meanwhile the body had to be protected from decay, which led to the arts of mummification, substitution by means of representation with copies of everyday objects, and the naming of things — spells to complete which, with the correct procedure, would ensure continued existence.

Dating Sources

One of the key problems in deciphering the timescale of Ancient Egyptian civilization is accurate dating. Needless to say, the Christian dating system did not yet exist; instead, the Ancient Egyptians dated by the regnal years of the current pharaoh. This could be further confused by the practice of co-regencies — developed as a means of ensuring succession and limiting the powers of other potential competitors. Some pharaohs dated their reigns from when they first came to the throne as a co-regent; others only when they began their own distinct reign following the death of their co-pharaoh. During at least three points in the history of Ancient Egypt, when centralized control broke down and the Two Lands fractured, there were rival pharaohs using their own dating systems, as well as other periods for which there are no surviving records.

A civilization spanning such a length of time — as well as one which measures that time by a different method to our own — poses difficulties in interpretation. Towards the end of Ancient Egyptian times, the society was absorbed by other civilizations interacting and expanding. In fact its very success and longevity coupled with its inherent archaism and isolation meant it was out-evolved by other more volatile, more interactive, Mediterranean societies — Hittite, Babylonian, and Persian, but chiefly Greek, then Roman — the precursors of our own civilization. Ancient Egypt eventually

Right: Gesso-painted wooden stele. At right a deceased man is being presented by hawk-headed Horus to Osiris, with the goddess Isis behind him.

Stelae were usually made of stone or wood; funerary stelae were left in or near tombs to inform both the gods and all who passed about the status and history of the deceased. They are, therefore, important primary sources and provide information about the detail of Ancient Egyptian daily life.

could no longer hold such forces in check and was absorbed by them — just as Greece and Rome in their turn underwent modifications, changing from polytheistic pagan religious beliefs, to semitically-derived monotheistic ones. Thus Ancient Egypt finally fell under the parameters of a verifiable dating system that extends up to the present day. This is one way we can trace a thread back to them, although the further back we go into their own system of dating with its "system crashes," the more tenuous and relative exact dating becomes.

Star Time

Another way of establishing the timescale is through what are known as absolute dates — the records of star time. The Ancient Egyptians knew of Sirius, (which they called Sopdet) basing their astronomical calendar upon its orbit. The Nile rose and began its inundation with the rise of Sopdet in the heavens.

In the Ancient Egyptian civil calendar, the solar year was divided into three seasons based upon the behavior of the Nile. Each of these three seasons was divided into four 30-day months, to which were added five festival days, making a total of 365 days. But the lack of a leap year every four years, to take account of the extra quarter of a day each solar year, eventually led the ancient calendar to become completely out of synchronization with the seasons, only returning to sync every 1,460 years when Sirius regained its original position. By searching all ancient sources and records for any mention of these helical risings of Sirius, and then calculating from historically-dated occurrences, we can get another fix on the Ancient Egyptian time-frame — although it still has a margin of error, which increases the further back we go, back eventually beyond records.

There are also other important primary archaeological sources — such as the archaeological remains of temples and funerary buildings, statuary, stelea, and papyrus documents. But these, by their very nature, are incomplete, and the interpretation of them by experts often varies. However, as time progresses the amount of research and data into such primary archaeological sites yields more and more. This, with progressive collating, leads to an incremental yet continuous increase in our overall knowledge of Ancient Egyptian civilization.

Other secondary sources exist, too — mainly observations of Ancient Egyptian culture by outsiders, more often than not Greek. Herodotus visited Egypt in 5BC, and although his observations cannot be taken as gospel since he was writing to entertain as well as inform and was prone to exaggeration, invention, and the recording of unverified facts and local myths, his observations nevertheless contain valid information.

A Greco-Egyptian priest named Manetho wrote an influential history of the country around 300BC, using ancient sources — some of which have not survived, just as his history,

too, has not survived in complete form to the present day, but is quoted by other Roman and Greek sources. Manetho lived at the beginning of the Hellenistic Ptolemaic period in which, following the decline of the indigenous monarchs, the native elite was gradually replaced by a Greek ruling class. These people still observed outwardly many of the old religious forms, just as the Romans were to do in an even more cynical fashion. Manetho split Ancient Egyptian history into three Kingdoms — Old, Middle, and New — separated by three Intermediate Periods, spanning some 30 recognized dynasties, stretching from around 3100BC down to the last indigenous pharaoh, Nakhthoreb (or Nectanebo II) in 343BC, a schematic that is still accepted today, though with reservations. Manetho obviously had access to a variety of sources, including official state and temple papyrus documents that have not survived, but he was prone to recording other popular folklore, exaggeration, legend, and hearsay. Some of his sources can be consulted today to check his veracity — these include the Rosetta Stone, the Royal Lists of Karnak and Abydos, and the Palermo Stone.

Even when all these different sources are combined, we still have gaps and margins of error which inevitably increase the further back in time we go, but by and large a sequence of events and pharaohs is possible, with a few misty patches (the Intermediate Periods, which the sheer length of time has worn to shreds).

The Canon of Turin

This is a papyrus dating from the

Left: Reliefs on a giant column from Kom Ombo with traces of original paintwork still visible. Such carvings are another important source of information, revealing myths and beliefs as well as recorded events.

reign of Ramesses II, inscribed in heiratic with the names of Egyptian rulers. Originally, there were about 300 names and it was virtually intact when first discovered. However, on arrival in Italy its condition had badly deteriorated. The list included the Hyksos rulers, although they were given a hieroglyphic sign which indicated they were foreigners. As well as a king list, there were some details about each reign, with occasional numbering alluding to dates since the time of the legendary founder of the country, Menes. Furthermore, there was an attempt to go back beyond mankind to the time when the gods ruled the earth, providing a vital link in Egyptologists' figuring of mythology.

Almost all the surviving king lists derive from religious and funerary contexts, usually relating to the cult of ancestor-worship, with each king trying to establish and prove his own legitimacy. Several exist, but only that of Seti I is still in situ. It is at Abydos: western museums have cornered the rest. There is, however, no absolutely definitive list intact.

Egyptian Concept of Kingship

At the apex of Ancient Egyptian society was the king, known to his subjects as *nesu*. The word pharaoh comes from the Greek translation of the Egyptian *per-aa,* meaning Great House, which first of all describes the palace, but later on came to symbolize kingship and the king. He was the head of state, in charge of the civil administration and the army, as well as being the chief priest of every god in the kingdom. He was also a divine being himself, the offspring of a god, his divine birth coming directly from his father, in whom God was incarnated.

The pharaoh was seen as an incarnation of Horus, the posthumous son of Osiris, the divine king slain by his brother Set. Horus fought his uncle to regain his father's kingdom and carry out the last rites for his father, who then became king of the underworld and afterlife. As in legend, so in reality: each pharaoh became Horus in life and Osiris in the afterlife, continuing the link between gods and mortals.

To ensure the succession, it was vital that all religious protocols were followed, during life and in the afterlife too. As the idea of kingship developed, so, too, did the preparations for the king's continued existence and harmony in the afterlife rely upon the correct approach, design, construction, maintenance, provision, and observance of the rituals required for that afterlife, and the smooth passage of all physical existence — from the sun rising and setting to the annual inundation and the prevention of entropy and chaos.

To this end, the idea of divine kingship was developed over the millennia, with giant constructions, lavish decoration, precise and intricate ritual, and the process of mummification — all coalescing into the reality of the immortal kingship of the pharaohs.

Right: The ancient and important deity, Osiris, king of the underworld, was usually portrayed mummiform and bearded, colored green, wearing the *atef* crown and holding royal symbols including the crook and flail. He dealt with death, resurrection, and fertility; manifesting deceased royalty, he emphasized the continuity of the royal lineage, with the living king described as his son Horus.

The Names of the Pharaoh

From around 2500BC onwards the pharaoh had a series of five names to identify him. The first was his Horus name, contained within a *serekh,* which was a representation of the facade of a palace with the falcon-god Horus perched on the top. This equated the pharaoh with Horus, who was legitimately awarded the throne by a tribunal of deities following his battle with his uncle, Set. This was the earliest sign of royalty, occurring on the Narmer Palette and even before in the proto-dynastic primary evidence at Naqada.

The second royal name was the *Nebti*, or two ladies' name, linking the king with the patron goddesses of Upper and Lower Egypt — Wadjet and Nekbet — and underlining his rightful claim to the kingship of both countries.

The third was the *Bik-nub* or Golden Horus name, whose exact significance has been much debated. Gold was the seen as the "flesh of Ra," perhaps further emphasizing the king's perfection and divinity, with the title also underlining the victory of Horus over Set.

Next came the prenomen or throne name, with the accompanying title "He of the Sedge and the Bee," (King of Upper and Lower Egypt). These names were all composed on the accession of the pharaoh, almost always incorporating the name of the great sun god Ra.

Finally the king had his own name given to him at birth, preceded by the title "Son of Ra," and sometimes followed as well by various epithets such as — "Beloved of Amun" (*mery-amun*) or "Divine Ruler of Thebes" for example. These last two royal names are the ones most commonly used, enclosed within a "cartouche"

Left: The incised cartouche of Ramesses II, containing his throne name: *User-Maat-Ra Setepen-Ra*, meaning "The justice of Ra is Powerful — Chosen of Ra."

(*shemu*) — an oval outline representing a double rope which eventually superseded the *serekh* as the ultimate symbolic container for the names of kingship (although it was not until later dynasties that this mode became typical: the earliest dynasties had only their Horus name coupled with their birth names).

It is from cartouches featured in various king lists, dating mainly from the New Kingdom period tombs and temples, that our knowledge of the sequence of the pharaohs is gleaned, along with a few other primary and secondary sources. It must be recognizd that each king list has been found to be different and incomplete; this is due to the loss of central control during the Intermediate Periods, to damage inflicted over time, and to politico-religious correctness that saw the removal from the list of the names of various rulers who were later deemed unsuitable, for whatever reason.

Ancient Egyptian Society

Just below the king was the class from which his royal family originated — the educated elite, a hierarchy consisting of nobles, priests, and civil servants, the highest-ranking of which were often (but not always) related to him. In earlier times the next highest official was the chancellor, but for the greater part of Ancient Egyptian history the senior official was called the vizier (*tjaty*). Sometimes there were two viziers — a northern and a southern one. Beneath these mandarins were numerous lesser civil servants responsible for religious protocol, the treasury, the armed forces, agriculture, irrigation, and all the numerous aspects of state. All of them bore the title of scribe (*sesh*) — a vital means of advancement in a world where literacy was rare and therefore empowering.

Beneath this educated elite was the vast majority of the population, involved mainly in agricultural production. However, given the Nile's cycle and the relatively small population in ancient times, it did not require intensive farming to produce a surplus, and there was always time during the growing season following the inundation to leave the fields and provide labor for the construction and upkeep of the key state buildings necessary for the realization and continuity of society.

The stupendous effort expended to construct these monuments required something more than intimidation: belief by the mass of the population in their own potential and the necessity of the enterprise —

Previous Page: Texts from a temple wall relief at Abydos.

Below: Statues of Prince Rahotep, a son of Snofru and High Priest at Heliopolis, and his wife, Princess Nofret, from their twin mastaba tombs at Maidun.

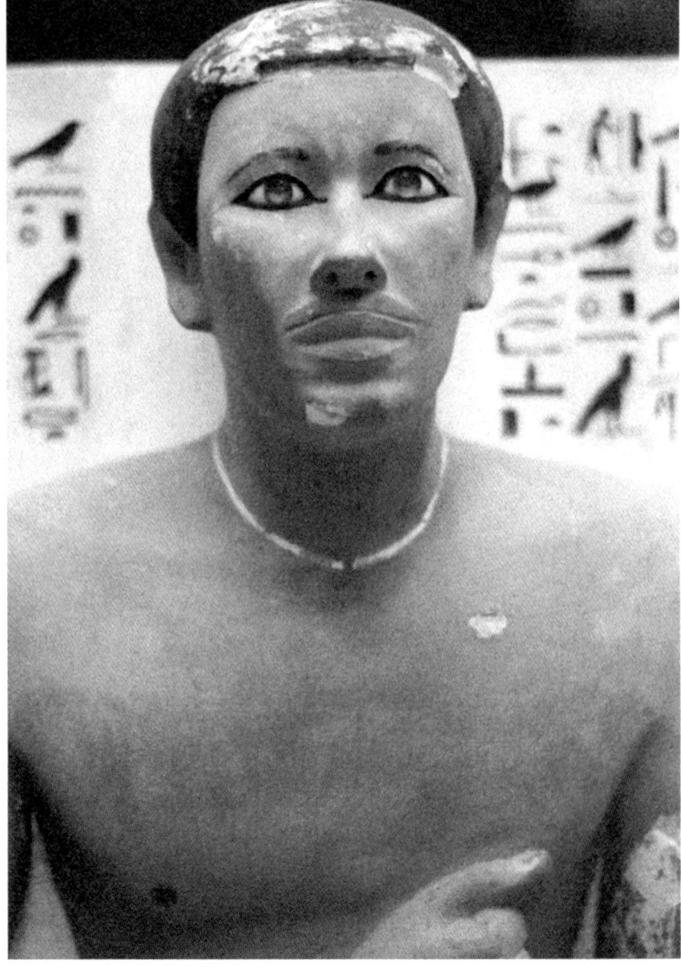

though over time they were sorely tested in their faith.

The fact is that Ancient Egyptian society was intensely religious and superstitious on all levels, with the supernatural closely interwoven with reality in many aspects of everyday life. Furthermore, as the state deities became incorporated into and indistinguishable from the government structure, so the primarily agricultural population coped with the everyday problems of life with recourse to magic, spells, charms, and folklore, appealing to the zooamorphic gods of each hazard to intercede on their behalf — local gods with the character of their locality. These, by their very nature, leave little trace for future generations to analyze, and for the most part archaeological evidence is more concerned with the fragments of monumental remains left behind.

Generally the lower strata of society worshipped local deities at their neighborhood shrines, these were often run on a part-time basis by the people themselves, who only joined the worship of state-sanctioned cults on the special festival days. The principal difference between the state and the private religion was that everyone had their own intimate relationship with the god of their choice, while the state religion was more concerned with the magical maintenance of society and the universe than with everyday thanks and supplication. There were meeting points and overlaps of the two worships, of course, with animal veneration, oracles, and festivals, in particular, crossing both categories.

The land was farmed by various individuals, groups, and state organizations, including the great temples dedicated to the state-sanctioned cults. These temples owned large tracts of land, and just as the church in European society grew wealthy through donations of land and produce, so too did the Ancient Egyptian

Above: A hierocephalous zooamorphic deity — one with the head of a god and the body of an animal — in this case the head of a hawk with the body of a crocodile. Most of the gods took on a feared or venerated animal aspect in the locality where they were worshipped.

temples come to rival the pharaoh in power and prestige, causing severe problems in the balance of that power and eventually leading to high priests who claimed kingship and became priest kings.

The idea of eternal life also modified over time, eventually even allowing for a certain democratization of the afterlife, with any, who had led a good honest life and who could pass Maat's test of truth and justice, capable of becoming an Osiris himself and joining him in the underworld. It was still accepted that the afterlife was, in fact, just like the present one only everlasting, which gives a clue to what the people thought of their life and their pharaoh.

The signs and emblems of kingship are revealed as latent or fixed already prior to unification, where there is already an established iconography, the crown, bulls tail, linen kilt, eye paint, Horus motif, serekh, smiting ikon, heraldic crests, standards, etc., and the beginnings of the hieroglyphic alphabet. These were developed and modified only very slowly as befits an archaistic society.

Whether Mesopotamian influence was as great as some experts intimate, Ancient Egyptian culture soon went radically its own way — the distinctive geography and environment of a desert-oasis country forced its own distinctive stamp on the people and their culture, and the Nile was a continuous thread linking communities, focusing life at its edges and forcing peoples to compete and compromise. It was definitely in the management of the river that society was forged, just as mummification was, perhaps, the result of a technique to recreate the natural results of arid desert burial.

Elements of the Body

To the Ancient Egyptians a person was made up of five elements, consisting of the name, the physical body, the *Ba*, the *Ka*, and the shadow.

The *Ba* is similar in concept to the modern idea of the personality, but it also conveyed power — it could cover gods and inanimate things. The deceased had to journey from the tomb to rejoin his *Ka* in order to be transformed into an *Akh*, and since the physical body could not do this, it was the duty of the *Ba*. The hieroglyph for this was made up of two animals whose phonetic values were the same as *Ba* — migratory birds were particularly seen as an incarnation of the *Ba*, although it could adopt any form. For bodies to survive they had to be reunited with their *Ba* every night.

Above: Ushabti figures are usually mummiform statuettes that were placed in tombs to answer for the deceased and perform any labor or menial tasks required. They were used to replace the costly live sacrifices that were the norm of the first few dynasties, with substitution by representation.

Ka is intrinsic life energy, human, and divine, which comes into existence at the same time at birth, and is portrayed as a mini-double. When a body died, the *Ka* continued to live, requiring sustenance — hence offerings real and figurative whose energy could be absorbed by the *Ka*. There are funerary statue images of the *Ka* often with its symbol.

The reunion of the *Ba* and *Ka* in the underworld transformed the deceased into an *Akh* — the form in which the Blessed Dead inhabited the region. Once created by the union of *Ba* and *Ka*, the *Akh* was eternal and was usually portrayed as a Ushabti-like mummiform figure. Its name was vitally important, as it gave clues to its date and geographical origins, as well as indicating an essential element of the whole person. It was also necessary for survival in the afterlife, as names were regarded as manifestations of named phenomena.

The symbolic importance of the *Akh* is witnessed by the removal of names and cartouches on tomb walls and monuments from disgraced persons: as the *Akh* symbolized protection and eternity, this was a way of eliminating the person entirely, including their memory and very existence.

Mummification

The preservation of the body was a vital part of Ancient Egyptian funerary practice, since it was back to the body that the *Ka* would return for sustenance. If the body decayed or was unrecognizable the *Ka* would go hungry, and so its afterlife would be in jeopardy: mummification was thus dedicated to the preservation of the body.

Ancient Egyptian religion had three basic aspects: the first two, the official state and mortuary spheres, are both well documented, supported by much archaeological evidence. These aspects took the form of observance of ritual and cult practices carried out by the pharaoh and the various priesthoods in temples that were off-limits to the rest of the population. In the earlier periods these priesthoods were usually related to the pharaoh. Inside, through correct procedure and observance, the gods took up residence in their images, and acknowledged and bestowed power on the pharaoh. Then, through him, they influenced society as a whole. It was only during festivals and special celebrations — although without actually seeing the images — that the public had access to the god and took part in the state-managed parades.

At his death, the pharaoh became one with Osiris and lived with Ra, and through his pyramid complex could live on with all his needs provided for — incarcerated with him was virtually everything he had in his earthly life copied, painted, and represented for the afterlife. The first pharaohs even had their wives and retainers buried with them, but this population-intensive sacrifice was soon substituted with representational figures, carvings, and paintings.

The preservation of the corpse itself became increasingly important and evolved into a complicated religious process — all part of equipping the pharaoh (and eventually the nobility) with what was necessary for an eternally happy and luxurious afterlife.

Along with pyramid building, mummification is the most famous skill of the Ancient Egyptians. It is a method of preserving artificially the bodies of dead people and animals, and evolved from the natural effect of desiccation that happened in the first simple graves of the Pre-Dynastic period. Bodies placed in shallow graves and covered with sand survived very well because of the arid atmosphere and intense heat. When graves became more elaborate, with coffins and vaults, these natural conditions changed and necessitated the development of preservation techniques and complicated ceremonies to ensure survival in the next world.

Mummification took place in workshops attached to the various necropoli, which also supplied most of the other funerary equipment. Methods varied according to time and location, as well as with the wealth and importance of the deceased.

By the Fifth Dynasty, internal organs were being removed, with only the heart left in place. The vacant body cavities were filled, and the outer wrappings were saturated in resin so that the features could be carefully modeled and then emphasized with paint. In contrast to earlier Pre-Dynastic burials, the body was laid in an extended position. By the time of the New Kingdom, these methods had evolved, with better preservative techniques on the tissues. At the peak of the art of mummification, the whole process took 70 days and the most vital part was the dehydration of the body in natron — a naturally occurring preservative.

Firstly the brain was extracted,

Below: The mummy of Ramesses II, that was found in the Great Royal Cache at Deir el-Bahari in 1881 and now rests in the Cairo Museum. His body is partially unwrapped and shows the remarkable state of preservation that the Ancient Egyptians were able to attain with their techniques.

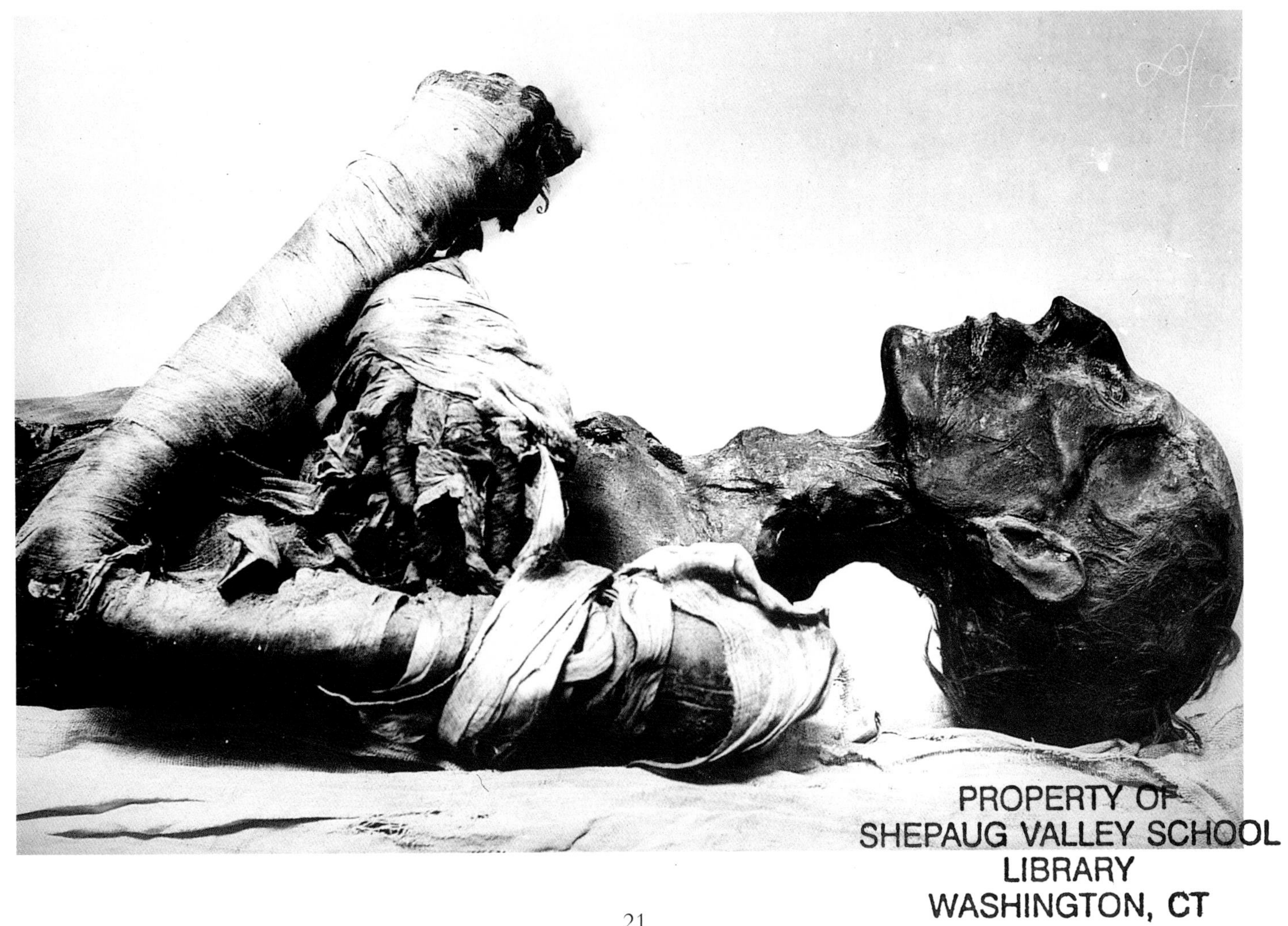

Left: The visible tops of Tutankhamun's canopic jars, fashioned in the young king's likeness. Canopic jars were stone or ceramic vessels made to house the viscera of the deceased which were removed prior to mummification. The four jars would contain the stomach, the liver, the lungs, and the intestines, each guarded by one of the four sons of Horus.

Right: The painted outer lid of a sarcophagus from the Greco-Egyptian Ptolemaic period, revealing the fusion of the two distinct styles.

Below: The burial chamber of Tutankhamun, with his solid gold inner coffin. On the walls of the chamber scenes from his funeral were painted, along with his successor Ay performing the "Opening of the Mouth" ceremony on the Osiris-form mummy, and the king being greeted by the goddess Nut. The western wall has extracts from the funerary *Book of Amduat*, along with 12 squatting baboons, representing the dark hours of night.

sometimes through the nose, but also through an incision in the skull. Next the viscera were removed through an incision in the left side, and then the cavities were sterilized. The viscera were treated separately with natron, then dried, and covered with molten resin. (Eventually the viscera and other parts were stored in Canopic jars, each guarded by a son of Horus and a protective goddess.) The body was now temporarily packed with natron and fragrant resins, before being immersed in natron for about 70 days. When this time had passed, the temporary packing materials were removed and sand and clay were used to bulk out limbs just underneath the skin. Next the body cavities were filled with resin-soaked linen, and bags of fragrant materials, herbs, and incense. Finally, the body was anointed with unguents and bandaged up with protective amulets and jewelry; the outside of the bandages were also often painted with a likeness of the deceased.

At the end of the 70-day period, and just prior to burial, a ceremony was carried out called the "Opening of the Mouth," in which the mummy was magically brought back to life. The mummy was then placed in a coffin, often anthropoid in shape, and again the image of the corpse was painted on the front. For the great pharaohs and nobles there was often a huge outer stone sarcophagus. Within coffins and on the walls of tombs were painted and written texts and spells to aid in the afterlife — the coffin and pyramid texts, and the *Egyptian Book of the Dead*. Eyes were painted on the sides so that all things

within the tomb could be activated by the owner.

Other items of funerary equipment included funerary statuettes, called *Ushabti* figures. The purpose of these was to have an avatar who could carry out any of the deceased's drudgery or unpleasant work in the next life. Sometimes there would also be a life-sized wooden statue of the deceased, or else a painting, so that the soul could inhabit this when necessary to obtain sustenance and move around, making use of the many grave goods with their replica images. In the afterlife with the gods, the owner of the tomb still had his own place, where he could rest and revive, before returning to the celestial environment.

Most mummies in the delta area of Lower Egypt have not survived, due to the damper climactic conditions. But in the more arid valley area of Upper Egypt, a large number have survived in very good condition and give us first-hand evidence of complicated burial techniques. Due to the high rate of robbery, and the official and unofficial destruction, pharaohs and priests both sought ways to safeguard the kings and their afterlife.

The best known method was by providing supposedly impregnable stone structures known as pyramids. The Ancient Egyptian word for pyramid (which is Greek) is *mer*, meaning "Place of Ascension." Eventually, probably during one of the Intermediate Periods of unrest and decentralization, the high priests decided to safeguard the bodies of the royal kings, and to this end moved them to deep-shaft caches, in the process of which some were damaged further, some lost their outer coverings, or lost their own sarcophagi and were placed within others. There were two big royal caches that have been found (so far): at Deir al-Bahari (in the Theban Hills) and Amenhotep II's tomb in the Valley of the Kings.

Below: The limestone outer enclosure wall of King Djoser's step pyramid complex at Saqqara. Originally a 32ft 9in (10m) high wall of bastions and recesses enclosed an area measuring 1,788 x 994ft (545 x 277m). The wall had 14 buttresses acting as false entrances; only this one in the south-east corner was a true entrance.

Aspects of Royalty

Heb-Sed Festival

This was the ritual of renewal and regeneration performed by the pharaoh after he reached his 30th year on the throne — although it seems that some pharaohs celebrated this festival much earlier. The two main elements of the ceremony were the acknowledgement and the paying of homage to the enthroned king, and the ritual of territorial claim. Some of the first evidence of this ritual is seen on an oil-jar label from the tomb of King Den at Abydos, in which he is shown running between markers that apparently represent the whole country.

It appears that the mortuary complex was where the pharaoh's *Heb-Sed* Festival was held. In Djoser's complex at Saqqara, there are a series of ritual buildings and courts, including two thrones symbolizing the Two Lands. In an adjoining court to the south, boundary markers were found and beneath the pyramid, on reliefs, Djoser was shown running, holding unidentified implements or regalia. Even though it eventually atrophied to representation in reliefs, this festival continued to be a vital part of the celebration of kingship. Following the first *Heb-Sed* they were held roughly every three years thereafter, as and when the pharaoh felt the necessity: the festival was obviously used to bolster his reign and underline his rule.

Above: The southern face of Djoser's step pyramid. Despite the missing white limestone casing and the hole in the superstructure, this first prototype pyramid is stunningly impressive — truly a tomb suitable for a god-king, designed and built with a brilliance and care seldom seen again.

Sekhem Scepter

The symbol of royal power, seen in the king's hand from the early dynastic period onwards, was the *sekhem* scepter, which also served as a badge of rank for high officials going about on royal business. *Sekhem* translates as power or might, and was sometimes incorporated into royal names, as well as that of the goddess Sekhmet — literally "she who is powerful." The pharaoh would usually hold the *sekhem* scepter in his right hand, with a mace or else a censer in his left. The scepter is also associated with Anubis, and the making of offerings to the *Ka* of the deceased.

A Short History of Ancient Egypt

A major feature of the early dynasties was the development of building in stone, and the obsession with the correct procedure for attaining life after death, both of which were destined to become lasting cultural habits. The kings of these proto-dynasties built *mastaba* — then multi-*mastaba* or stepped tombs — at Naqada, Abydos, Saqqara, and Helouam — including the legendary Imhotep's step pyramid, the earliest stone building of its size in the world.

By about 3500BC, as has already been discussed, two large kingdoms had emerged called the "Two Lands": Upper Egypt, stretching from the first cataract of the Nile at Elephantine (modern Aswan) to the edge of the Delta; and Lower Egypt, comprising the Delta area itself. Upper Egypt was known as the White Land, with its capital city at Nehken (Hierakonpolis), near Edfu. The kingdom's deities were the hawk-headed Horus, and the vulture goddess Nehkbet, and the king wore the tall White Crown. Lower Egypt was called the Red Land, with its capital city at Pe, (also called Buto). Here the king wore the Red Crown, and the cobra-goddess Wadjet was worshipped, along with the composite animal god Set.

These two kingdoms were finally united around 3100BC, yet their origins were never forgotten. They were, rather, celebrated in the title of the country and the king, who wore the new Double Crown (known as the *Shemty*) which combined both the Red and White Crowns, with their respective protective goddesses included. Because of its location on the Mediterranean, the delta was the meeting point for trade, immigration and technology from the continents of Asia, Africa, and Europe, whilst the south, except for Kush (Nubia), was much more insulated from outside influence, and consequently retained its traditions and culture intact for considerably longer.

From the time of Scorpion and

Narmer, (the original uniters of the two lands) succeeding pharaohs undertook military campaigns within the country to maintain the integrity of the state. When they felt secure they began to venture further, to keep back the savage nomads who came from the deserts around them, and search for the precious materials they needed for building and decoration — principally turquoise, stone, ivory, gold, and timber.

The Fourth Dynasty, ushered in around 2575BC, saw the golden age of the pyramids of the Old Kingdom; there were major advances in the fields of art and architecture as well as trading expeditions to Nubia. During this time, it was believed that only the pharaoh received everlasting life, though everyone else could take part through their contribution of service to the pharaoh, both while he was alive in this world and when he went on to eternity. Thus the construction of the royal pyramid complex became the focus of the entire society, of vital importance to everyone — the pharaoh and his subjects — and vast resources were used to achieve this aim. The cycle of inundation and growing allowed for a large labor surplus with which to build the vital monuments of state.

Also at this time there was an attempt to rationalize the incredible number of gods and the consequent wide variety of religious beliefs, into a more cohesive and manageable whole. As the larger cities became great religious centers in their own right, so various deities merged or became linked in groups or "families," each with its own distinctive, yet similar, creation myth. The largest cities at the time were Memphis, Heliopolis, Hermopolis, Nekhen, and Buto.

By the Sixth Dynasty the Old Kingdom was beginning to succumb to its own limitations; there was too great a centralization of power, too much tax pressure on farmers, and too many resources were being used in the building and maintenance of huge funerary complexes. The priesthoods and local governors had become very wealthy and powerful at the expense of the pharaoh, and gradually the country broke back down into its provincial beginnings.

Above: The Giza pyramid field, featuring those of Khufu, Khafra, and Menkaura, along with the subsidiary pyramids of Menkaura's queens. The Great Pyramid was built by Khufu, though due to its construction on slightly higher ground the second pyramid, built by Khufu's son Khafra, seems the larger. The smallest of the three main pyramids belongs to Menkaura.

The First Intermediate Period saw the Two Lands splintered, with foreigners entering the Nile Delta, alongside a rapid change and high turnover of pharaohs. During this time of upheaval, religious beliefs and customs inevitably underwent dramatic changes too. With the idea of the god-king discredited, people now wanted to enjoy their own personal eternity, and as a consequence the god Osiris, and the redemption he offered, rose to prominence.

There was a minor Hierakonpolitan resurgence in the Ninth and Tenth Dynasties, but they were overwhelmed by a new Theban line, which reunited the country, leading to the Middle Kingdom period. Montu, the Theban god of war, became dominant, before giving way to Amun in the Twelfth Dynasty. This was a period of expansion, immigration, and trade. There were campaigns in Nubia to keep the vital gold routes open, and a lot more contact with outsiders coming into the Nile Delta; expeditions were made to Punt and into Sinai. The country was reorganized and land reclamation schemes pursued, the highlight of which was the reopening of the ancient irrigation system, repaired to its former glory.

The pharaohs of this Twelfth Dynasty tried to reduce the power of the local nobility, with the aim of establishing the dominance of Thebes. While Amun was the main god, the pharaohs supported other cults too: Ptah at Memphis, Hathor at Dendera, Min at Coptos, Re-Atum at Heliopolis, Sobek in the Faiyum, and Osiris at Abydos. There was also increased democratization of the afterlife — a result of the universal appeal of Osiris.

At death, regardless of personal wealth or position, the departed was judged in the presence of Osiris by 42 assessor gods, and the deceased's heart went on the scales opposite the weight of Ma'at's feather of truth and justice. Passing this test guaranteed eternal life with Osiris, and there was consequently a much wider distribution of non-royal tombs and an increased range of funerary equipment.

The Second Intermediate Period came about again through weak rulers and simultaneous dynasties competing from their different bases at Thebes and from the Delta at Xois. This internal confusion enabled Middle Eastern outsiders, the Hyksos, to come pouring into the delta and, for a time, they took over almost the whole country. Their leaders became pharaohs, and they adopted local gods and traditions (with the unfortunate choice of Set as their main royal god). The Hyksos brought with them various technological innovations — in arms, construction, metallurgy, and agriculture, but relations between them and the indigenous population soured.

There was another resurgence at Thebes, in the Seventeenth Dynasty, which finally managed to expel the foreigners, and set the stage for the final flowering of Ancient Egyptian civilization: the New Kingdom of 1570–1085BC. Now Egypt was no longer isolated but an important part of the busily competitive ancient Mediterranean world. There was a demand for trade and, just as important, to establish borders and zones of Egyptian control and influence.

The pharaohs of the Eighteenth Dynasty by these means expanded their country and built an empire — conquering Palestine, reaching as far as the Euphrates in Syria, securing the delta to both east and west with fortifications, penetrating south as far as the Fourth Cataract of the Nile, and

Below: View of the facade of the hypostyle hall at the Temple of Hathor at Dendera, a Greco-Roman period temple which was never completed. It remains one of the best preserved of all Egyptian monuments, partly because it was buried in sand until the mid-nineteenth century.

securing control of the Nubian gold mines. Egypt was asserting itself in the face of increasing competition from Libyans, Hittites, Sea People, Nubians, and all the other tribes and groups pushing each other onwards in the restless development and exchange of early civilization.

Soon other greater waves would overwhelm them, too, but for now Egypt had an empire. With 2,000 years of history and experience already behind her, she was the wealthiest country in the world, with tribute pouring in from all corners. The capital was at Thebes, and the air god Amun was combined with the creator sun god Ra into the supreme state god Amun-Ra. His magnificent temple complex at Karnak became the most powerful religious and political center in the empire. Eventually, through this power, the priesthood would come to wield such influence as to control the royal line of succession and turn Egypt into an ecclesiastical state.

The tombs of the pharaohs were hidden in a valley (the Valley of the Kings) where they were cut into rock, as they eschewed the pyramids that were so easily robbed and desecrated. Their families and followers were once again buried nearby in their own necropoli.

The Eighteenth and Nineteenth Dynasties saw a fantastic increase in construction all over the country. Some of the best-known pharaohs achieved this status because of the vast wealth at their disposal, and therefore the sheer number of monuments and buildings, temples, forts, tombs, and statues bearing their names.

In recognition of their successes the pharaohs heaped treasure on Amun-Ra, but, as his priesthood became increasingly rich and influen-

Left: View along part of the main axis of the temple complex at Karnak; the gigantic red granite obelisk just before the hypostyle hall is the remaining one of a pair raised by Thutmose I.

tial, the pharaohs had cause to regret it, and tried to curtail their power.

One method the pharaohs adopted to circumvent the priesthood was that of co-regency, when an elderly pharaoh had his heir already acknowledged and active in his government.

Perhaps Akhenaten (originally Amenhotep IV) and his attempt at monotheism with Aten, was using a ploy to break the power of the priesthood of Amun-Ra. If so it failed, for Aten had no popular acceptance and was too abstract a deity to appeal to the masses; when Akhenaten died, Aten went with him and the old gods were restored.

By the time of the Twentieth Dynasty a high proportion of land had passed to the temples and into the control of the priesthood — especially that of Amun at Karnak — to the point where the priests controlled nearly the whole of Upper Egypt. The priesthood itself became

Above: Another view of the huge temple complex at Karnak; built over 1,500 years it was renowned throughout the ancient world for its size and wealth of adornment. From the Middle Kingdom onwards it was constantly added to and embellished. Finally it was sacked by the Assyrian king Ashurbanipal circa 667BC, a devastation from which it never managed to recover. The religious and city center then moved about a mile away to the south to Luxor.

Left: A bronze figure of Amun-Ra, ultimately the supreme god of the Ancient Egyptian pantheon, wearing his complicated double-plumed and sun disk crown, symbolizing his sky/star origins.

hereditary and so completely independent of the pharaoh that it was able to form its own dynasty, which became strong enough to rival the state itself. Within the royal line, too, there were conspiracies and jostling for position that only served to weaken the whole succession. There were strikes among the royal workmen;

dissatisfaction and unrest spread throughout the land. Finally, when the throne fell to a high priest, Lower Egypt defected and Nubia broke away; the nearer eastern possessions had already been absorbed by the expanding Hittite and Babylonian nations.

The Twenty-First Dynasty ruled from Tanis in the Nile Delta, with only token acknowledgement from Thebes. Gradually, relations between the two improved enough for intermarriage to take place between the royal and hereditary priesthood lines, until the two became united in form, if not reality.

The Twenty-Second Dynasty ruled from Bubastis in the Delta and was of Libyan extraction, but after an initial increase in prosperity, there was a period of conflict and decline, with numerous simultaneous local dynasties — the Twenty-Fourth at Sais in the Delta, and the Twenty-Fifth, a Nubian line, recognized as far as Thebes. Both the institutions of pharaoh and priesthood were severely weakened at this time.

After an initially prosperous start, the Twenty-Fifth Dynasty came into conflict with the newly-emergent and territorially aggressive Assyrian power that was expanding eastwards. At first held at bay, the Assyrians finally took Memphis in 671BC, and drove the pharaoh south, from where he briefly counter-attacked. But by 650BC the Assyrians were in control, ruling through a noble line from Sais.

Eventually, however, Assyrian domination was cast off by the pharaohs of the Twenty-Sixth Dynasty, which had started in 668BC during the period of struggle. A new development at this time was the use of Greek mercenaries in military campaigns — a usage that increased over the next three centuries. The city of Naucratis was specifically given by the Egyptian authorities to Greek mercenaries and their hangers-on, specifically to prevent the intermingling of foreigners and Egyptians.

As Assyrian power waned, the Babylonians and Medes filled the vacuum, and Egypt was forced into making an alliance with its old enemy and erstwhile possession, the Palestinian states, in an attempt to balance this latest threat. But in 539BC Babylon itself was overthrown by a newly emergent power — Persia — which, once it had conquered Babylon, looked to invade Egypt. Following the siege and fall of Memphis in around 520BC, the pharaoh was put to death and Egypt became a Persian satrapy.

Some Persian kings were more highly motivated than others in their rule over the Two Lands, but by and large the country was ruthlessly exploited with very little being put back in return. Uprisings were pitilessly suppressed, and the Egyptians were forced to tolerate Persian rule as there was simply no other alternative.

As soon as the opportunity arose there was an immediate appeal for help, and once again Egypt had recourse to Greek military aid, this time from the city-state of Athens. Despite the peace treaty between Athens and Persia of 449BC, there was only a short period of freedom for the Twenty-Eighth, Twenty-Ninth, and Thirtieth Dynasties, before the Persians savagely reimposed their rule in 343BC. They were to remain in power until Alexander the Great swept their empire away.

Alexander took Egypt without bloodshed and was widely welcomed

Below: The remains of Akhenaten's city of Akhetaten, situated at modern Tel el-Amarna. The city was systematically destroyed by traditionalists seeking to expunge the Amarna interlude from history. Because it was subsequently unoccupied, it reveals much about the plan and layout of an original Ancient Egyptian town.

Left: After the devastating defeat and death of the Persian King, Darius, Alexander the Great was welcomed as a savior by the Ancient Egyptians. He journeyed to the oasis at Siwah to consult the oracle, where he was confirmed in his status as a living god.

Below: Harpokrates, a Greco-Egyptian version of the young Horus. According to legend he was the child of the goddess Isis, being portrayed in human form, sometimes with a child's sidelock, a finger to his mouth, and seated on his mother's knee. As a naked god-child he possessed various healing and protective powers.

as a savior; and, as in all his conquests, he behaved with foresight and compassion. Local traditions and culture were tolerated and religious freedom encouraged. He hoped to bind his vast empire with common ideals of mutual freedom and respect. Had he lived, no doubt his approach would have had far-reaching effects. In the short time he was in the country, Alexander reorganized the government, mainly in the military and financial departments; he accorded the gods particular respect, and travelled to Siwah, the distant oracle of Jupiter-Amun, where he was

acknowledged by the god and therefore won acceptance from the native population and eventual deification.

With Alexander's death, Egypt fell to his most able general — Ptolemy — who founded a dynasty that spanned 250 years, and saw the Hellenization of much Egyptian culture. The exchange, however, was by no means all one way. The Ptolemeic pharaohs adopted the Egyptian tradition of royal brother-sister marriage. They restored and built temples in the traditional manner, and created a hybrid Greco-Egyptian god — Serapis — a combination of aspects and elements belonging to Osiris, Zeus, Helios, and Aesculapius.

Under the Ptolemaic pharaohs the Greeks spread out across the country from the cities of Alexandria and Naucratis; they also colonized the fertile Faiyum, an oasis with a large lake fed by the Bahr Yusef, a branch of the Nile that diverges from the main river to the west. The abolition of the old Egyptian aristocracy paved the way for the creation of a new, predominantly Greek, nobility. There was the occasional native uprising, especially in the area of Thebes, but these were always easily suppressed.

The only real danger to the Ptolemeic succession came from within itself — caused by constant internal bickering and struggles for succession. Furthermore, alongside this Hellenization there was growth and increased sophistication of sculpture, and also a huge increase in animal worship — grown out of a direct overlap of Greek and Egyptian religious cultures.

The dynasty ended with the famous Cleopatra, that artful queen who strove vainly with all the means at her disposal to protect her country from Roman dominion. But it was not to be, and with her death Egypt became little more than the granary of the Roman empire — exploited without compunction. Only the occasional emperor showed any personal interest in the country, with barely a token acknowledgment of Egyptian cultural processes. Unlike other provinces of the Roman empire, Egypt was given no autonomy, but was governed directly by the emperor through a prefect.

The Romans followed the example of the Greeks in accepting and adopting the titles of "Pharaoh and Divine Son," since it gave them the legitimacy to rule, and so to exploit Egypt for Rome's benefit. But the native culture continued among Egyptians until the advent of Christianity. Rome, too, eventually succumbed to Christianity, having fought unsuccessfully to suppress this new religion, and, finally, in 311AD Constantine, the first Christian emperor, issued the Edict of Tolerance, effectively converting Egypt to Christianity.

During Emperor Constantine's reign, Christianity spread throughout Egypt, and the government was reorganized into a diocese of six provinces. There were persecutions of pagans and heretics; the old gods and their temples were attacked and the old faiths were destroyed. However, it was not until AD540, that the last temples (on the island of Philae near Elephantine) were closed, and the ancient gods of Egypt, after almost 4,000 years, died.

Far Left: Relief at the temple of Hathor at Dendera of Cleopatra with her son by Julius Caesar — Caesarion, who replaced her brother Ptolemy XIV, whom she murdered on her return from Rome following Caesar's death. Caesarion was killed by Octavian after her defeat and suicide.

Left and Below: Trajan's Kiosk and the Temple of Isis on Philae Island at Aswan. The temple was a comparatively late foundation, the earliest remains so far discovered dating from the Twenty-Fifth Dynasty (747-656BC). In Roman times the Temple of Isis became the premier pilgrimage destination for worshippers of the cult of Isis. The complex also has the distinction of being the last functioning temple of the Ancient Egyptian religion, which struggled on until it was closed down by edict of Byzantine Emperor Justinian in AD551.

Trajan's Kiosk (also known as the "Pharaoh's Bedstead" because of its shape) was designed as the formal entrance to the temple complex. It is open to both the east and the west and was never completed, possessing unfinished walls and only a few reliefs.

THE PHARAOHS

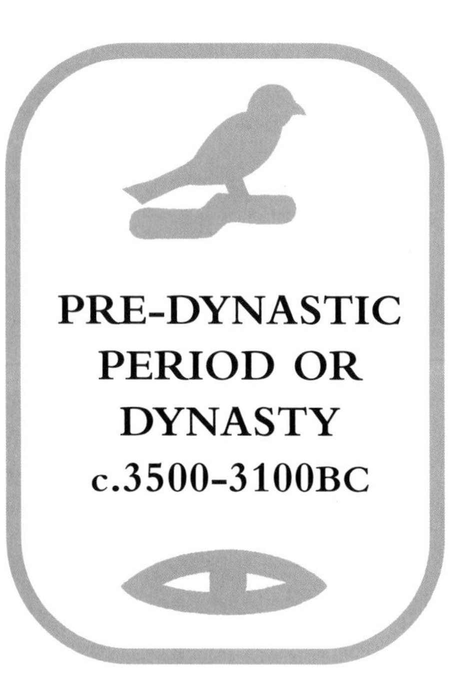

PRE-DYNASTIC PERIOD OR DYNASTY c.3500-3100BC

The recognized beginnings of pharaonic Egypt saw the unification of the two large states of Southern and Northern Egypt, both of which had struggled into existence by the agglomeration of various smaller units. That unification finally happened is undisputed, but who finally achieved it is more uncertain.

It would seem there are at least two candidates — Scorpion and Narmer. From ceremonial remains found in a pit named the "Main Deposit" at Hierokanopolis (Nekben) the final unity of the two lands is confirmed, with its inherent duality celebrated in the king's titles and the use of the northern Horus motif to signify overlordship. The various palettes and maceheads show the historical event of the unification idealized in pictograms, with Scorpion and Narmer both personally identified. Possibly they are the same person, but it seems more likely that they are both being celebrated as holders of the office of "Unifier." Apart from his name on a palette nothing further is known about Scorpion.

Narmer was also known as Menes, meaning "Establisher," making him a good candidate for being the founder of the unified state, although — as with the term "Unifier," other pharaohs were also called this. Perhaps it was Narmer who saw the strategic necessity for moving the capital and founding Memphis. His queen was Neithotep, a northern princess, the alliance with the southern Narmer helping to cement the bond between the Two Lands.

The iconography also displays the celebration of the duality of the Two Lands. The religious primacy was of north over south: the northern Horus dominated the southern Set, and Horus would become hugely significant to the pharaohs. Military domination was quite the reverse: the south beat the north and the kings of the first dynasties came from This, or Thinis, the early capital town of the victorious south, whose precise location remains unknown. They were buried in the necropoli at Abydos.

Hor-Aha

c.3100BC

Hor-Aha succeeded Narmer to the throne. He was possibly his son or some other close relation with knowledge and power about the throne. He took the Nebti name "Men" meaning "established," and is therefore a candidate for the Menes of legend as well as the previous Menes/Narmer. His two names — Hor-Aha and Men — appear side by side. Hor-Aha continued his predecessor's work to establish the Two Lands as a single state, with campaigns fought north and south, but his lasting achievement, was the founding of Memphis, or Hutkaptah (sanctuary of the *Ka* of Ptah).

The founding of Memphis was vital to the strategic survival of the Two Lands, furthermore by building a huge dyke, the city was protected whilst at the same time gaining vital river-access — this proved critical. Memphis would only decline in importance with the later supremacy of the Theban dynasties.

Hor-Aha's tomb is located at Abydos, next to that of Narmer. It consists of a sunken complex of three chambers that were originally roofed

Overleaf: Wall relief showing the *pschent* or *shemty*, the Double Crown symbolizing the unification of the Two Lands. This was made up of a combination of the two crowns of Upper and Lower Egypt: the White Crown or *hedjet*, a tall conical head-piece ending in a bulb, and the Red Crown or *deshret*, a coil protruding from a throne-like arrangement.

The unification crown consisted of the two headresses combined by the insertion of the conical White Crown into the Red Crown, with the addition of a *uraeus* (cobra and/or vulture) on the front. The Double Crown was thus complete, and was called "The Two Mighty Ones."

Below: The calcite sphinx at Mit Rahina, where there was the massive temple complex of Ptah, the city's chief deity, as well as the embalming house of the Apis bulls and a palace of the pharaoh Merneptah. Little is left now, except this famous sphinx and some statues of Ramesses II, along with a few tombs of the high priests of Ptah dating from the First Intermediate Period.

in wood. Slightly to the east of the main structure there is evidence of sacrificial satellite burials. Also close to him is the tomb of his probable queen, Neithhotep.

Djer

c.3000BC

Djer, Manetho's Athothis, succeeded Hor-Aha. Perhaps he was also known as Iti, mentioned in the King List at the temple of Seti I. Around his tomb at Abydos are some hundreds of satellite burials implying the accompaniment of his retainers to provide for him in the Afterlife.

Human sacrifice would not figure large in pharaonic burials with the religious advance of replacement by representation. Small painted wooden or clay Ushabti figures, called "anwerers," took over from real human sacrifices. There were also larger statues of the king, imbued with power through magic to become a vehicle for the sovereign's *ka*, his spiritual double.

There is also evidence of military campaigns during Djer's reign, something that was again to become a feature of kingship. To keep everything and everyone in order, military expeditions were necessary — and, when fought against primitive tribesmen, they required only regularity to drum home the message.

The king's wife, Herneith, was buried at Saqqara in a tomb next to other nobles of the period. In later periods Djer's tomb was thought to be that of Osiris and a cenotaph was built there.

Djet

c.2980BC

The acknowledged successor of Djer, although a list has been found along with another large tomb at Abydos which implies a queen regent first — possibly Mereneith, consort of Djer.

Djet, too, pursued a military policy with enthusiasm, establishing the supremacy of the new monarchy. He also celebrated his jubilee with a *Heb-Sed* festival. His tomb is different from his predecessors, built and laid out in a more deliberately formal manner, using a lot of stone for the first time. There is a masterfully bold *serekh* on a funerary stele now in the Louvre, containing Djet's Horus name. Djet's chancellor was named Hemaka, he had a large tomb at Saqqara signifying his importance.

Den

c.2950BC

With Den (also known as Udimu), the historical records become stronger and the mist shrouding the early monarchs begins to clear through the correlation of various records — the Palermo Stone, Manetho, and the Abydos King List, as well as the many inscriptions and labels from tombs at Abydos and Saqqara citing the king and events during his reign.

His was the first reign in which a monarch began to use the *nebti* name in the royal titles and the first recorded instance of the king wearing the Double Crown. It is also the first instance of the "smiting icon" and of a campaign against Asiatics in the east.

There was initially some confusion about the location of Den's tomb, with it being mistakenly attributed to large remains at Saqqara; these were eventually attributed instead to his chancellor, Hemaka. Though of inferior quality, Den's tomb is at Abydos.

Anedjib

c.2925BC

Anedjib, is also called Miebidos by Manetho, who attributed 26 years to his reign.

There is some evidence that during his reign there were dynastic struggles between rival royal families of the north and south. Anedjib came from This and is called a Thinite king in the Saqquara King List. There was also at this time the beginnings of combination northern and southern funerary styles that would eventually lead to the pyramids. His tomb at Abydos is one of the smallest and worst constructed, with its burial chamber made entirely of wood. There are also a few satellite burials of a similar standard. Some of Anedjib's funerary equipment had his name defaced and replaced with that of his successor.

Semerkhet

c.2900BC

It seems likely that Semerkhet was not related to Anedjib and usurped the throne on that king's death. This is implied by his omission from the Saqqara King List which indicates some kind of political or religious incorrectness.

On official records carved into the Palermo Stone, Semerkhet reigned for nine years, although he is attributed 18 years by Manetho who also says there were numerous disasters during his reign. His tomb at Abydos is of a far higher quality than Anedjib's, though no other tombs attributable to his reign have been found anywhere.

Qa'a

c.2890BC

Not much is known about this final pharaoh of the First Dynasty. His tomb at Abydos had at some indeterminate period undergone various enlargements and alterations, with the thick brick walls of his burial chamber eventually hollowed out to make storage magazines. There are also only a few satellite burials; these come to an end with his reign.

A stele bearing his name enclosed in a *serekh,* with a white crown indicating southern supremacy, was found in the environs of his tomb. Various other tombs at Saqqara have been tied to his reign, including one that seems to have a prototype mortuary temple, the forerunner of more complicated burial processes.

SECOND DYNASTY 2890–2686BC

Manetho's history records that the Second Dynasty consisted of nine kings who ruled a total of 302 years, but archaeological evidence does not support this, and current opinion gives this dynasty five rulers who ruled for approximately 200 years. The sequence of the first three has been found on the back of a kneeling statue of a priest called Hotep-dif.

HETEPSEKHEMWY

c.2890BC

Hetepsekhemwy is a nebulous pharaoh about which almost nothing is known. There is no evidence that this king used Abydos, but some remains and seals discovered close to the pyramid of Unas indicate that he might have been buried at Saqqara. Manetho states that he had a long reign of 38 years, but there is little or no evidence to support or deny this.

RANEB

c.2865BC

Raneb ruled for 39 years according to Manetho, yet there is almost no archaeological evidence to support this. Once again, tell-tale sealings near the pyramid of Unas hint at where his tomb once lay, and there is also a granite stele found at Abydos with his name within the *serekh*. Manetho says that it was Raneb who introduced the worship of the sacred goat of Mendes at Heliopolis and the Memphite Bull Apis, but this is now believed attributable to Den's reign.

NYNETJER

c.2825BC

Nynetjer ruled for 47 years according to Manetho. The Palermo Stone records facets of his reign, including feasts, the running of the Apis bull, and military campaigns — eastwards as well as northwards into the Delta, indicating continued disturbances or else the necessity of regular displays of military might to impress onlookers. Also recorded was the birth of his son, Khasekhemwy, who would become pharaoh after Seth-Peribsen. In fact jar-sealings bearing his name have been found near the Giza necropolis, indicating that his tomb was perhaps one of the very first in that area.

SETH-PERIBSEN

c.2750BC

His tomb at Abydos has sealings bearing both the names Sekhemib and Seth-Peribsen, the former surmounted with the Horus insignia of royalty and the latter with Set. It seems that he came to the throne with the name Sekhemib, but during his reign the rivalry between the Two Lands, (which had occasionally manifested in previous reigns) erupted into open conflict once again. This is evinced by the dropping of his Horus name in favor of a Set name: Seth-Peribsen. The struggle was obviously of a politico-divine nature, and he perhaps sought to appease all parties, or the supporters of Set and the north held sway; whatever the reason, Horus was replaced on his *serekh* with the composite animal god Set.

KHASEKHEMWY

c.2685BC

The conflict between the two elements of the country continued into the next reign. With Khasekhemwy, however, this contradiction is partially resolved when this king made the diplomatic move of combining both Set and Horus above his *serekh*. Did Khasekhem change his name to Khasekhemwy (meaning "The Two Powerful Ones Appear"), after he had put down rebellion in the north, as a gesture of acknowledgement?

Evidence has been found to confirm that before the peace the northern insurgents had almost reached Nekhen (Hierakonpolis). The rebellion must have been serious to reach so far and it is recorded that there were almost 50,000 northern casualties. When the conflict finally ended, Khasekhemwy married a northern princess, named Nemathap, to cement a new bond between the Two Lands. He also placed the northern god Set above his *serekh*, accompanying Horus.

Khasekhemwy died in around 2686BC, equipped with a massive tomb that is unique in its size and shape. Although it was robbed in ancient times there were a few artifacts that were missed, including the king's golden scepter.

Below: Wall painting of Horus from Dendera.

THE OLD KINGDOM 2686–2181BC

THIRD DYNASTY 2686–2613BC

With this dynasty Ancient Egyptian culture began its first great flowering, known as the Old Kingdom. It saw continued military expansion and increased trade, with advancements also in art, technology, and architecture. The incredible pyramids — a fusion of southern and northern burial styles — were conceived and constructed. The rationale of the monarchy also underwent change, in order to weld the Two Lands together, with greater emphasis placed on the divine nature of kingship — the king was the living manifestation of Horus, and a son of Ra.

There is a view that the Old Kingdom represents the very first and highest peak of a dynamic evolution, and from then on, for over two thousand years, there was simply a slow descent. To realize this brilliant phase, everything coalesced into a complex multi-faceted system of belief and representation, with magic and military might mixed in. Such a highpoint couldn't last: even the Nile sometimes did not deliver. The constant growth in costs of the mortuary complexes and pyramids became a heavy drain on resources; add the dynastic squabbles and power struggles to the increasing separatism of the nobility in the provinces, and the end result — political and social fragmentation — is hardly surprising.

Sanakhte

2686–2667BC

Also known as Nebka. Sanakhte reigned for approximately 18 years, about which very little is known. He is thought possibly to have been the brother of Djoser, the next pharaoh and author of the step pyramid at Saqqara. Sanakhte still had internal political problems to deal with as well as exterior campaigns. The remains of a red sandstone relief from the Sinai attest to the king's eastern campaign with the familiar "smiting ikon." This era certainly saw the ever increasing development and exploitation of the Sinai's mineral wealth which consisted mainly of copper and turquoise.

Djoser

2667–2648BC

Known to his contemporaries as Netjeriket, the name by which he is described on all his monuments, Djoser ruled for 19 years. He was the famous instigator of the first stone building in the world — the magnif-

View from inside the incomparable Step Pyramid complex of Pharaoh Djoser. Imhotep, the architect, was accorded the unheard of honor for a commoner of inclusion with his king, being mentioned by name. He was later deified.

icent step pyramid at Saqqara — along with his vizier and chief architect Imhotep, who was accorded the honor of statues in the king's tomb, thus to be a companion in the hereafter. Imhotep, portrayed as a bald-headed scribe, was later deified himself.

Within the step pyramid structure is the groundplan of Ancient Egyptian religious thought: the pyramid itself was conceived as being the sacred power source and thus the heart of a complex that essentially linked society to eternity, the stars and cosmic unity, and the continuity of the sun's daily journey across the sky bringing life to all. The Ancient Egyptian word for pyramid — the Greeks ironically called after the shape of the little wheaten cakes they ate, was *Mer*, or "Place of Ascension," the linking chamber between the two worlds of life and death. This first pyramid is a series of *mastaba* tombs piled up on top of each other. Various alterations and adaptations were made while it was being built, revealing the experimental nature of the project. The end result is that the pyramid is riddled with shafts and corridors — some made by robbers looking for treasure, others that were made for members of the royal family.

The mortuary complex laid out tombs, temples, and chapels, a *heb-sed* court for celebrating the king's jubilee, symbolic houses of north and south representing the unity of the Two Lands, and a *serdab,* to allow the king's *Ka* to gather sustenance from the food that would be placed on the altar outside. There were reliefs on all the walls and the whole complex was surrounded by a high wall with 13 false doors and only one true one.

The step pyramid is such a magnificent achievement that it would have taken a less powerful king much longer.to build. It is a testament, above all, to the organizational ability of the Ancient Egyptians, developed through communal irrigation schemes and other such co-operative ventures, and completed with almost no technology other than mounds and rollers. The art of pyramid building represented at least the equivalent mystique and relevance of later Christian churches and temples.

Netjeriket had to put up with the inevitable internal north-south unrest that continued to simmer, for it was not just the Libyan, Kushite, or Bedouin tribesmen that needed a display of pharaonic might: the Two Lands needed continuous political and military effort to remain in existence.

Manetho states that there were a further six kings in the Third Dynsasty, who ruled for a total of 157 years. However modern opinion tends toward a further three, with a joint span of approximately 36 years.

Sekhemkhet

2648–2640BC

Until comparatively recently there was almost nothing known of Sekhemkhet. There are various rock carvings in one of the Sinai desert wadi attributed to him, including a "smiting icon" of him, proving this dynasty's continued interest and exploitation of the area. Then, in the early 1950s, traces of a huge enclosure wall and the remains of a first massive mastaba step were found — an unfinished step pyramid which would have had seven steps and would have been taller than Djoser's. However, when the sarcophagus was finally extracted with its original sealings intact, there was no trace of the king. Sekhemkhet died after a short reign of six years, not long enough to complete his monument, and his body has not been found so far.

Khaba

2640–2637BC

Khaba, the successor to Sekhemket, had a short reign of only three years. It seems he did not use Saqqara. Instead, his pyramid is situated a mile south of Giza. Again, as with Sekhemket's edifice, it was intended to be a six- or seven-step pyramid, though it also seems never to have been used. Traces of sealings and vases bearing Khaba's name found in mastaba tombs nearby have tied this structure to him, but it seems that it was never used and his body has never been found.

Huni

2637–2613BC

The last known king of the Third Dynasty as given in both the Saqqara King List and the royal Canon of Turin papyrus, Huni reigned for about 24 years. He, too, did not use Saqqara but moved his burial site to Meydum, near the Faiyum, 50 miles from Giza. It was the first pyramid to have a square ground plan and be geometrically true, with the steps packed out and then the whole edifice faced in limestone. Today there remain only three steps, and the present shape has resulted from the partial collapse of the outer skin.

Meydum became the basic groundplan for future pyramid complexes, consisting of the pyramid itself, containing a north-facing entrance which descends to a burial chamber. On the east side of the pyramid is another smaller one, possibly a mortuary temple, and from this a causeway runs down to the edge of the cultivated habitable area where the valley temple was located. In some of the tombs of the nobles buried near their master are exquisite wall paintings and other works of art that reveal the level of artistic achievement of the society at that time.

The severe and majesterial figure of Nesu Netjerikhet, also known as King Djoser. This life-size, seated *Ka*-statue originally sat in the *serdab*, a place without doors but instead with a few eye-holes so that his *Ka* could receive tribute and offerings from worshippers or leave the chamber if it so desired.

Considerably more primary evidence of the Fourth Dynasty survives than of earlier dynasties. The Manetho version quoted by Eusebius says there were 17 kings who spanned a total of 488 years; however the Manetho version given by Africanus gives eight kings and 277 years. Current opinion gives this dynasty six kings reigning for approximately 120 years. Like their predecessors, the kings of the Fourth Dynasty were from Memphis, but sprung from a different royal line.

SNEFRU

2613–2589BC

Also known as Sneferu and Snofru, Nebmaat, and also the Greeks as Soris. Snefru was a son of Huni, the last king of the previous Third Dynasty, but by a minor secondary queen or concubine, named Meresankh. His suitability was further enhanced when Snefru married Hetep-heres, the daughter of a more senior queen.

The Palermo Stone records Snefru's campaigns and expeditions beyond the borders of Egypt. He journeyed to the Lebanon to collect cedar wood, timber being such a scarce resource within Egypt that it was constantly sought from outside. He mined the Sinai for turquoise and launched military strikes against the Nubians in the south and the Libyans in the west. He also moved the royal burial site again — to 28 miles north of Meydum. Here he built two pyramids, about which there has been considerable debate. The northern Red pyramid is the first true pyramid built, and was probably where Snefru was buried, with his wife's tomb nearby. The tremendous resources required to build both these structures, as well finishing a third for his predecessor, implies a great degree of stability and control. Snefru consolidated the Two Lands into a single entity, and was able to hand on a strong inheritance to his son Khufu. He was also celebrated in later literature as a good humored and beneficent ruler.

KHUFU

2589–2566BC

Also known as Cheops and by the Greeks and Romans as Suphis I.

The authors who quote Manetho all agree that the successor to Snefru was Khufu, whom they called Suphis.

Khufu reigned for about 24 years, with the usual military campaigns, and resource-gathering missions, but his lasting achievement was to build one of the Seven Wonders of the World, the oldest and the only surviving one as well: the Great Pyramid at Giza. For 4,500 years, until the 19th century it was the tallest man-made structure (originally 481ft/146.6m, but now 451ft/137.5m.)

Khufu also relocated his burial ground, this time to the Giza plateau, putting all his efforts into a single monument, though curiously he did not choose the highest ground. (This was left to a later king, Khafra, whose pyramid would consequently seem taller to the naked eye, though it is in fact smaller). The great pyramid underwent several internal modifications, but its exterior dimensions were decided and held to from the outset. Herodotus wrote that the causeway leading to the pyramid took ten years to build, and the pyramid itself 20. But the time taken and the manpower needed are unknown to us, as is the exact method of construction. Ironically, the only remaining image of the builder of such a huge edifice is a tiny ivory statuette. Also near and round the Great pyramid were two other momentous discoveries: a boat pit with a full-sized intact ship contained within, and the tomb of Khufu's mother, Hetep-heres, containing furniture of wonderful quality and design.

DJEDEFRA

2566–2558BC

Also known as Radjedef, Djedefra was the son of Khufu, though his reign was brief and, as his tomb remains are difficult to interpret, little is known about him. It seems he too moved his burial site, and also changed the layout of his complex, which never progressed much beyond the initial laying-out stage. His main significance is that he added "Son of Ra" to his royal name, a practice that would become standard with later pharaohs.

KHAFRA

2558–2532BC

Also known as Suphis II and Kephren, Khafra was another of Khufu's sons, Khafra was the builder of the Second Pyramid and, probably, the Great Sphinx at Giza. Manetho identifies him as Suphis II, with a reign of 66 years. The Canon of Turin papyrus gives him 24 years, which

Several boat-pits were found close to Khufu's Great Pyramid at Giza, with at least two found occupied. One has been the subject of intense restoration and is now housed in its own museum close by. This solar barque was available for Khufu's use in the afterlife and has revealed much about the ancient building techniques: including the use of ropes instead of nails, which were then soaked to expand and seal the holes.

seems more likely and is supported by evidence in a mastaba tomb nearby his own tomb. Whatever the truth, Khafra's reign was long enough to complete a stunning funerary complex, which was to become the archetype of Old Kingdom tombs. It consists of a valley temple set on the edge of the cultivated area, with a causeway leading into the desert and the western horizon of Osiris. Khafra built his pyramid on higher ground than his father, giving it the illusion of being the larger. It does, however, still

Far Left: Close-up of the massive limestone blocks that make up the internal structure of Khufu's Great Pyramid. Some 3,200,000 blocks were used, averaging 2.5 tons each.

Left and Below: Two views of the Giza pyramid field showing Khufu's Great Pyramid and Khafra's with its 'snow-capping' of white limestone. Originally all the pyramids would have been encased in this white stone, with their granite apexes (called pyramidions) sheathed in gold or electrum.

possess some of the white tura limestone at its apex, giving an idea just how majestic these buildings must have been when complete.

The Sphinx is an integral part of Khafra's funerary complex, carved and built up from an outcrop of slightly imperfect stone — the reason it was left by the first quarrymen. A crouching lion with the face of the pharaoh — it represents Ra-Harakhte, the manifestation of the sun-god at his rising in the east. For much of its life it has been covered by the sands, though it has been cleared at various times, revealing a temple between its front paws and a stele commemorating the restoration carried out by Thutmose IV, following a dream he had while still only a prince.

MENKAURA 2532–2503BC

Also known as Mycerinus, Menkaura succeeded his father Khafra, and reigned for approximately 28 years, although Manetho gives him 63. His pyramid is considerably smaller than the others; perhaps precisely because of the size and effort of his predecessors, he decided to forego the struggle of building so large a tomb and instead used the resources elsewhere. Indeed, it's possible the building of the previous two pyramids had used up almost all resources; if so, we shall never know. His pyramid was originally intended to be only 100ft (30m) tall, but was expanded to a final height of 228ft (70m). The shape of the coffin found there in the 1920s did not correspond with other Old

Though the word sphinx is Greek, it is thought to be a transliteration of the Ancient Egyptian *shesep ankh*, meaning "living image." The Great Sphinx at Giza is thought to bear the face of Khafra, whose pyramid is alongside. It has spent much of its life covered by sand and has undergone various reconstructions. A Fourth Dynasty temple was found between its paws when they were uncovered.

Above: A distant view of the Giza pyramid field.

Left: Close-up of Khafra's pyramid showing the cap of original limestone cladding that still remains.

Kingdom culture and was probably an attempt on the part of the later Saite monarchy to piously restore a desecrated tomb. Many slate statues of an exceptional quality survive of Menkaura; these were found when his valley temple was cleared early this century. His queen, Khamerenbty II, a daughter of Khafra, was buried in the larger of the three accompanying smaller pyramids that lie alongside Menkaura's.

SHEPSESKAF
2503–2498BC
Menkaura had an eldest son, Khuenra, who must have predeceased him, for he did not succeed to the throne. Instead, Menkaura was succeeded by Shepseskaf, another son by an unknown queen. He had a very short reign of only four years.

The Fourth Dynasty's fortunes, it seems, had taken a turn for the worse and, perhaps as a consequence, Shepsekaf moved his burial site, returning to the old royal burial ground at Saqqara. He did not attempt a pyramid but built a tomb in the shape of a large rectangular sarcophagus.

More pictures of the Giza pyramid field. Though traces of First Dynasty mastaba tombs have been found at Giza, it is predominently a Fourth Dynasty cemetery. The famous triumvirate of pyramids belong to the Fourth Dynasty rulers Khufu, Khafra or Kephren, and Menkaura, which, along with the Great Sphinx, have brought Giza lasting fame.

FIFTH DYNASTY 2494-2345BC

The origins of the Fifth Dynasty, as recorded in the Westcar Papyrus, are Heliopolitan. Manetho claimed that it originated from Elephantine but, as with much of his information, the closer it is scrutinized in the light of verifiable facts, the more questionable it becomes. What is known is that these kings of the Fifth Dynasty came to acknowledge the ascendancy of Ra over the other gods. This is evinced from their now badly battered and ruined funerary complexes that reflect a religious change in emphasis. The sun became a more important focus for the funerary cult than before.

USERKAF

2494–2487BC

Also called Weserkaf, Userkaf, was the grandson of Djedefre, the short-lived successor of Khufu. His mother was queen Neferhetep, and he married a

The pyramids of the Fifth Dynasty pharaohs have been ruined. It was found that one, at least, had been hurriedly capped off to become a mastaba tomb. Once the casing had been stolen to be used in other buildings, the badly built internal cores soon broke back down into piles of rubble.

daughter of Menkaura, Khentkawes, uniting the two lines of Khufu.

Beginning with Userkaf, the Fifth Dynasty kings moved their burial sites back to the ancient royal burial ground of Saqqara, with Userkaf placing his pyramid complex, of which very little now remains, next to that of Djoser.

Because they accorded far more importance to the sun-god Ra, the Fifth Dynasty pharaohs are known as the sun-kings.

Userkaf took the unusual step of moving the mortuary temple of his complex to the south side instead of the usual east side. Userkaf also built a series of sun temples that were to become a feature of Fifth Dynasty kings, consisting of an altar and an obelisk on a podium, surrounded by an enclosure wall linked by a causeway to a valley temple, with a boat of Ra buried close nearby.

A colossal pink granite head of Userkaf, three-times life size, was found in the temple court. It is the only example of massive Old Kingdom statuary that has so far been found.

Sahura

2487–2475BC

Sahura was possibly a brother of Userkaf. His pyramid complex lies slightly to the south of Userkaf's, along with the later kings Neferirkara and Nyuserra.

His pyramid is the largest and his complex the best preserved, though now only a mound of rubble, his mortuary temple reveals wonderful carvings of high quality and the remains of beautiful friezes on its walls which offer some of the earliest pictorial evidence of Egypt's foreign military campaigns and trade. The ancient name for his pyramid complex was "The *ba* of Sahura gleams," as it must have done with the original white limestone shining in the sun.

Neferirkara

2475–2455BC

Also known as Kakai.

Neferirkara was probably another brother of the founder of the dynasty. His pyramid complex is almost completely ruined, lying alongside Sahura's at Abusir. The main innovation of lasting significance on this king's part was the introduction of a second cartouche (a royal name-containing cylinder), enclosing his birth name, Kakai. This would become common practice and helps distinguish between kings with similar or even the same names.

It is also from the remains of his mortuary temple that the earliest traces of hieratic script have been discovered. Lists of temple accounts, work rosters, and equipment lists all from the Fifth and Sixth Dynasties provide valuable information concerning funerary cults

Shepseskara

2455–2448BC

The remains of Shepseskara's unfinished pyramid complex lie to the north-west of Sahura's pyramid at Abusir. It seems that his reign was not long or prosperous enough to complete the complex. All the pyramids of the sun-kings of the Fifth Dynasty had such weakly built rubble cores that once the outer casing of white Tura limestone had been plundered, the core inside did not long survive.

Raneferef

2448–2445BC

Raneferef's incomplete tomb has been recently discovered in the Fifth Dynasty's Abusir burial site. His unfinished pyramid was capped off and turned into a *mastaba* tomb, probably by his successor. Also found in the remains of his mortuary temple were another collection of Fifth Dynasty papyri, seals, royal sculpture, and other artefacts which have yielded information about this little-known dynasty.

Nyuserra

2445–2421BC

Also known as Ini, Nyuserra's pyramid complex has been found alongside his predecessors. Like almost all others from this dynasty, it also is in a ruinous state providing scant information about this king. It seems Nyuserra appropriated his predecessor Neferirkara's valley temple and causeway, diverting it to his own complex. This constant recycling and reuse of monuments went on throughout Egyptian history. Fragments around the site show the remains of what must once have been brilliant painted reliefs. Some of these have been partially reassembled to show the celebration of the king's *heb-sed* festival, and also the omnipotence of the great sungod Ra.

Menkauhor

2421–2414BC

Also known as Kaiu.

Menkauhor was the last of the Fifth Dynasty kings to use Abusir. His pyramid complex, too, is now sadly a decomposed mass of plundered ruins, about which very little can be deduced at Saqqara . It is in fact from the tomb of a high official of the reigns of the last kings of this dynasty that some information can be gleaned. His name was Akhtihotpe and he was overseer of the pyramid towns of Nyuserra, Menkauhor, and Djedkara. His beautiful *mastaba* tomb, covered in reliefs and paintings that vividly bring to life the joy and plenty of Nile living and the added luxury of high rank, hint at what his kings' complexes must have been like.

Djedkara

2414–2375BC

Also called Isesi, Djedkara was the king who moved the royal burial ground back to Saqqara. A bedraggled 80ft (24m) heap of rubble on the edge of the plateau denotes his pyramid. Little else survives beyond the usual fragments of what must once have been fine reliefs. In fact it was not until his funerary temple was excavated that Djedkara's name could be definitely attributed to the ruins of the pyramid complex. At his father's death, Akhtihotpe's son, Ptahhotpe, became the overseer of Djedkara's pyramid town; he later shared the *mastaba* tomb of his father. In the ruins of Djedkara's mortuary temple, full-sized limestone and wooden statues of foreign captives were found. It is known from other sources that during his reign a pygmy was brought from the land of Punt, who caused a sensation when he was produced at court.

UNAS
2375–2345BC

Also known as Wenis, Unas was the last king of the Fifth Dynasty, the core of rubble that remains of his pyramid lies just to the south of Djoser's step pyramid, though the remains of the complex as a whole are discernible. His pyramid has the distinction of the being the smallest built during the Old Kingdom period, but the first one which was decorated internally, with the spells for the afterlife known as the Pyramid Texts.

A small piece of the causeway leading to his complex has been restored and roofed over with light permitted through horizontal slits, the walls are covered in paintings and carved reliefs showing scenes from daily life, painted with their usual exuberance and eye for detail. On the south side of the causeway lie two huge stone-lined boat pits. Unas' pyramid underwent repairs during the Nineteenth Dynasty, by Khaemwaset, a prince and son of Ramesses II who pre-deceased his father.

It seems that Unas left no heir to succeed him, which led inevitably to the instability. Into the vacuum stepped the next man of the moment, Teti, who became the founder and first ruler of the Sixth Dynasty.

SIXTH DYNASTY 2345-2181BC

According to Manetho, the Sixth Dynasty kings hailed from Memphis, and this is supported by their choice of burial sites at Saqqara overlooking their capital.

TETI 2345–2323BC

Also called Seheptawy.

Teti married one of the daughters of Unas, named Iuput, thereby legitimizing his claim and calming the political instability that had arisen with the heirless death of Unas. He adopted the Horus name of Seheptawy — "He Who Pacifies the Two Lands" — the first of many pharaohs to do so, to symbolize the restated unity.

Teti also allied himself to important nobility by marrying his daughter Seshseshet to the vizier Mereruka. Manetho states that Teti was murdered by his own bodyguard, although there is no other corroborating evidence. He seems to have reigned for about 12 years and continued the trade with Nubia and Byblos begun by his predecessors. His ruined rubble pyramid lies at the northern edge of the Saqqara plateau, the much damaged burial chamber containing various pyramid texts upon its walls. To the north lie the two smaller pyramids of his queens Iuput and Kawit, and the *mastaba* tombs of his courtiers. His chosen successor was his son Pepi.

USERKARA
2323–2321BC

It seems that Teti's son Pepi was briefly usurped by Userkara, who, because of the boy's young age, was able to intercede and seize the throne, albeit very briefly. Alternatively he was merely a regent for a time. Almost nothing is known about this shadowy king, although his name links him with the Sixth Dynasty.

PEPI I
2321–2287BC

Also known as Meryra. It is from a corruption of Pepi's name that the name of Memphis derives. He was the son of Teti and Iuput, who came to the throne young and enjoyed a reign of some 50 years. Perhaps his mother was his regent until outmaneuvered by Userkara.

During Pepi's reign the rise of provincial nobles accelerated; many had won increased wealth and position from supplying the funerary complexes, temples, and cults of deceased pharaohs, while doing the same for the current king. This brought tax exemptions and riches, along with royal friendship and patronage. These nobles could now afford to build fine tombs for themselves in their own nomes in Upper Egypt. This process of power leaking away from its center was to continue throughout the Sixth Dynasty.

Pepi's pyramid, lying at south Saqqara, is badly damaged, although surviving fragments reveal that it must have been of very high quality. It was the first pyramid discovered by archaeologists with funerary texts painted inside, although later discoveries would place it in a more correct timeframe. From the temple at Nekhen (Hierakonopolis) come two exceptional copper statues, one of the king and a smaller one of his son Merenra, now in the Cairo Museum. It seems from some of the records that there was some kind of harem conspiracy later in his reign which was discovered and quashed. He then married two daughters of a local prince and official from Abydos, both confusingly named Ankhnesmerire. One of them was the mother of Merenra, and the other the mother of Pepi II.

Merenra

2287–2278BC

Also known as Nemtyemsaf I, He succeeded his father for a reign of nine years. The son of the second Queen Ankhnesmerire. It is possible he had a brief co-regency with his father Pepi, because he kept Weni as his Governor of Upper Egypt, whom his father had already appointed. Merenra sent Weni to Aswan to cut five canals in order to ease the transportation from the quarries there of granite, to be used in the construction of his pyramid. The resulting pyramid is sited close to his father's in south Saqqara, with a star-spangled vault in the center. It seems that Merenra died in his prime; his sarcophagus was made of greywacke slate and the body found within is presumed to be that of the king, making it the oldest royal mummy to have survived *in situ*.

Pepi II

2278–2184BC

Also known as Neferkara, Pepi II succeeded his brother at a very young age, so initially his mother, Ankhnesmerire, II would probably have acted as regent, along with her brother the vizier Djau. Pepi married several times: Neith, daughter of his father and a half-cousin, Ipwet, and another niece, the daughter of his brother Merenra. His reign was the longest in Ancient Egyptian history. It witnessed the decline of central power and the rise of the nobility in the nomes, who cut impressive tombs for themselves as they were no longer willing to merely share their overlord's burial site. Their wealth did not reach the king, and heavier demands on Egypt's foreign interests further accelerated the political collapse.

Also at this time trouble broke out in Syria and Palestine, limiting the revenue from the east. To compound Pepi's problems, it seems that at the end of this period there were failures of the Nile in its annual inundation, with the consequent rise of famine and disease to accelerate the decline of the Old Kingdom.

Pepi's tomb is the last one of any size in the Old Kingdom. When he died, it is possible he was succeeded briefly by his son, Nemtyemsaf II, who was crown prince. But the Old Kingdom was finished and the country sliding towards civil war. Some sources (Manetho and Herodotus), mention a successor to Pepi II called Merenra II or Nemtyemsaf II, along with his wife, Queen Nitocret, who in turn succeeded him, but there is no archaeological evidence to support this. No doubt someone tried to hold onto power at Memphis, but its influence became increasingly local. With the demise of this Sixth Dynasty the period known as the Old Kingdom came to an end, and a more confusing decentralized period casts a veil that makes this time still more occluded.

THE FIRST INTERMEDIATE PERIOD 2181–2055BC

After almost a thousand years in which Ancient Egyptian civilization had burst out of the mists of time into the stunning glory of its artistic, architectural, and organizational/religious achievements, the breakdown of justice was a shock that underlined the fragility of the Two Lands. For the next 140-150 years chaos reigned. With the death of Pepi II, centralized control of the Two Lands broke down.

The historical sources of this period are inevitably confused. Manetho mentions a Seventh Dynasty of 70 kings that ruled for 70 days, but this is obviously an analogy for the chaos that ensued. Both the Seventh and Eighth Dynasties were Memphite, and they tried to claim and enforce a jurisdiction they obviously did not possess. Thebes, too, lost to Herakleopolis in the southern oriented power struggles. Accompanying this breakdown of centralized Memphite government arose the nomes, fighting for themselves and regional dominance.

Left: Hapy was the god of the Nile in flood and, therefore, the god of fecundity. He is recognized by the crest of papyrus on his head and is shown as an hermaphrodite.

These dynasties contain numerous ephemeral kings, who are known only from the King List at the temple of Seti I, at Abydos.

WADJKARA

The only king of the Eighth Dynasty for whom there is any real evidence. His Horus name was Demedjitawy. There is some evidence of numerous tax exemption decrees to various temples and nobles.

QAKARA IBY

A small pyramid belonging to Qakara Iby, close to the complex of Pepi II, is all that remains of this pharaoh. It is indicative of hard times as it is pitifully small and completely ruined Though decorated with pyramid texts, it exhibits none of the panache of the Old Kingdom.

The first successful challenge to Memphite central control came from Herakleopolis, just south of the Faiyum — an area that was to grow in importance and influence throughout the remainder of Ancient Egyptian history.

The Ninth Dynasty came from Herakleopolis, and possibly controlled the whole country for a short period, but by the beginning of the Tenth (and second Herakleopolitan) Dynasty some 30 years later, the southern nomes had banded together and dual sovereignty had become established. Eventually, southern Egypt was controlled by a royal line from Thebes that would become the Eleventh Dynasty. Open warfare broke out often between these two nomes. The border between the two occurred at Abydos which was swapped in conflict at various times by the two sides. This state of affairs continued until the Two Lands were reunited by the kings of the Eleventh Dynasty.

Both the dynasties from Herakleopolis were patently unstable, with frequent changes of ruler as incessant power struggles ensued. Also there was famine at different times which only added and encouraged this time of instability and anarchy. A few strong nobles held on to power in their local areas, as the country was, in essence, feudal.

Manetho mentions various kings who cannot be substantiated with any archaeological evidence. The first name found with its dual cartouche royal names is that of Khety Meryibra.

Right: We have little information on the pharaohs of the Seventh to Tenth Dynasties. However, the tomb of Seti I at Abydos has in it a room known as the Hall of Ancestors, which lists the 76 previous rulers beginning with Narmer. Interestingly, rulers who were "questionable," such as Akhenaten and Hatshepsut, are omitted from the list. This is the outside of Seti I's tomb.

KHETY I

Also known as Akhtoy I and Meryibra, Khety I initially gained power over almost the whole country following his violent usurpation of the Memphite monarchy. However, he was soon restricted to the lands north of Abydos as the southern nomes united under Thebes and began to fight for their own independence.

KHETY II

Also known as Akhtoy II, it is not known whether Khety II was a son or brother of the previous ruler, or just someone who assumed the name for legitimacy. Due to the fragility of a country locked in civil war, the few records remaining are vague and haphazard. All the Ahktoys of the Hierakleopolitan nome tend to merge together as evidence becomes more and more fragmented.

NEFERKARA

Also known as Ankhtify, Neferkara was nomarch of Hierakleopolis, and the successor of Khety II. He led a coalition of his own and the Edfu nomes against the southern Theban alliance. By this time the country had become a series of nome alliances formed into states that were jockeying for position and dominance.

KANEFERRA

It is recorded in the tomb of Ankhtify, the nomarch of the Herakleopolitan nome that he fed his famine-struck populace on the orders of Kaneferra. Other than this fragment, there is no other current evidence for this king.

There are brief mentions of other kings including Khety or Ahktoys III to V and Merykara, but evidence to differentiate between them or bring their names to life is impossible. So far, time has hidden them from us.

Mentuhotep I, although not a pharaoh himself, was the father of Intef I and, although he ruled the Theban nome, it was a time of truce between the rival alliances. This truce did not last for long and the struggle broke out again. It is his son who is accorded the honor of being the first pharaoh of a united country. However, in the reign of Senusret I, both Mentuhotep and his son Intef I were recognized as the founders of the Middle Kingdom.

INTEF I

2125–2112BC

Also called Sehertawy, Intef fought against Herakleopolitan hegemony with his father, Mentuhotep, finally taking the title Supreme Chief of Upper Egypt. Later on after he had made a secret alliance with the city of Koptos he beat back the Herakleopolitan alliance and took some rival cities. He then adopted a royal title.

INTEF II

2112–2063BC

Also known as Wahankh, whether he was the brother of Intef I or some other family member, Intef II was able to consolidate the gains of his predecessor and achieved a measure of control over Upper Egypt. He pushed the border still further north almost to Asyut. A stele outside his tomb records his border being the Tenth nome, Antaeopolis, beyond the Eighth nome of Abydos. Inscriptions in a tomb at Elkab detail a famine that took place in his reign.

INTEF III

2063–2055BC

Also known as Nakjtnebtepnefer, Intef III had a fairly short reign, which began with an uneasy peace between the two rival factions. This was maintained despite famine raging through the land.

His son and successor perhaps served a co-regency with his father.

All three Intefs aspired to control of the Two Lands, as evinced in their Horus names, they also reverted to the ancient *SEREKH* to contain their names rather than the cartouche, They were all buried in huge tombs in the Dra Abu-el-Narga, an area to the north of the Theban plain, close to what would become the Valley of the Kings. The design of these tombs has been labeled *saff,* meaning row, given because of their lines of porticoes and doors.

Right: The supreme creator god, Amun grew in importance after he had ousted Mentu, the Theban war god. Amun would go on to become the ruler of the Theban Ennead and come to lasting prominence as the chief god of the pharaohs from the Eighteenth and Nineteenth Dynasties. Amun was not just a god for the ruling classes: the poor venerated and revered him as a protective deity to whom they could appeal for fair play against corruption and manipulation from those above them, against venomous creatures, and protection on long journeys.

THE MIDDLE KINGDOM 2055–1650BC

The first Intermediate Period finally came to an end with the reunification of the country under the auspices of the fourth king of this Eleventh Dynasty, a dynasty begun merely as the ruling family of the Theban nome, and its first three kings were just that. But with their growing power came more territory, until they surpassed Herakleopolis and came to the point of being capable of the task of reunification.

Mentuhotep II

2055–2004BC

His birth name incorporated Mentu, war god of the Theban nome, although he was also known as Nebhetepra.

It was at Asyut, the border he inherited from his predecessor, that Mentuhotep fought for the big prize: complete unity and an intact country once again. This was finally attained some years into his reign, and gave rise to the changes in his Horus name. Initially it was "He who gives heart to the Two Lands," then "Lord of the White Crown," and finally "Uniter of the Two Lands."

The first part of Mentuhotep's reign saw the uneasy truce between the two sides gradually reach breaking point. The watershed in the civil war came in the 14th year of Mentuhotep's reign when the Thinite nome of Abydos rose in a revolt which began the final struggle for reunification. A mass grave of some 60 southern soldiers close to his tomb indicate the importance and extent of their sacrifice.

Mentuhotep finally took the cities of the Herakleopolitan alliance and become the undisputed leader of the re-united the Two Lands. To mark his victory he took a new Horus name.

Mentuhotep reigned for approximately half a century, and after the early years of discord and war, following his victory there was a gradual increase in peace and prosperity. He built his tomb on the west bank at Thebes, in the bay of cliffs at Deir-el Bahari. The design was unusual and innovative: a giant stepped podium with square-cut pillars and on the next terrace a hypostle hall at the base of the cliffs. In the plain in front of the temple is the entrance to a deep tunnel that leads to a chamber beneath the temple itself, which contained an impressive seated stone statue of the king wearing his *heb-sed* cloak and the Red Crown.

Mentuhotep built extensively in the original area of the Theban kingdom, beginning the meteoric rise of the town of Thebes, that would in time become a capital city.

Mentuhotep III

2004–1992BC

Also called Sankhkara.

His father's long reign enabled his son Mentuhotep III to inherit a prosperous and stable kingdom, though it also meant that he was quite elderly when he finally came to power. Consequently his reign was fairly brief — some 12 years.

Mentuhotep carried on his father's policy of securing the country's borders by policing both in the south in Nubia, and in the north at Sinai and Byblos. At the same time he also continued to develop trade. He carried out numerous building works with their consequent material-gathering expeditions for wood and stone. It seems that Mentuhotep was buried in the same bay of cliffs as his father. Some fragments have been found that intimate this, though no actual tomb has been discovered.

Mentuhotep IV

1992–1985BC

Also known as Nebtawyra.

Mentuhotep IV is given as the last king of the Eleventh Dynasty by both the Saqqara and Abydos King Lists.) But the Royal Canon of Turin papyrus says that there was a period after Mentuhotep III's death of about six years, and it is this period that is attributed to Mentuhotep IV. Records of him are sparse. His vizier was named Amenemhat, the same name as the first king of the Twelfth Dynasty. Perhaps they are the same man? It is also recorded that Amenemhat went with an army of 10,000 to Wadi Hammamat to fetch a fine block of stone. Perhaps he kept his army and took the throne, going on to found a new dynasty.

Manetho claims the Twelfth Dynasty consisted of seven kings who originated from Thebes; present opinion tallies with this, plus the addition of one queen — Sobeknefru, at the end of the dynasty.

AMENEMHAT I

1985–1955BC

Also known as Sehetepibra, the first king of the Twelfth Dynasty was the former vizier of Mentuhotep II. Amenemhat, it seems, was the son of a priest named Senusret, who was of Theban origin. It is from this dynasty onwards that the inexorable rise of the composite god Amun-Ra takes off. Amenemhat reigned for 30 years and brought stability to Egypt, laying the foundations of a dynasty that lasted for 200 years and whose passing would unleash the Second Intermediate Period.

After Amenemhat's enthronement, he cruised the length of the Nile, crushing all opposition to his rule, launching military campaigns against both Nubians and Asiatics, in the course of which he extended the borders of his country. He also apparently moved his capital to some 20 miles south of Memphis, creating a fortified city which he named Itj-tawy or "Seizer of the Two Lands." Although this has never been found, it is thought to be somewhere in the region of modern Lisht.

Amenemhat's reign brought much change, including a re-organization of the administration and the introduction of a period of shared kingship called co-regency, which all the Twelfth Dynasty kings would practice, probably as a way of safeguarding the succession. Thus in the 20th year of his reign he acknowledged his son Sunusret, and they shared the throne for a decade until Amenemhat's murder. During this time the younger man handled the more active roles of kingship, including the military campaigns and internal policing. Amenemhat's murder at the hands of unknown assassins reflect some partially failed coup. Amenemhat also moved the royal burial ground to Lisht, at the entrance to the Faiyum, and built his pyramid to a design similar to those of the Old Kingdom.

SENUSRET I

1965–1920BC

Also known as Sesostris I and Kheperkara, Senruset came to inherit the throne following his father's murder, which took place whilst he was co-regent away on a campaign against the Libyans in the western desert. He hurried back and stamped out the coup and buried his father. He then enjoyed a reign of over 30 years, witnessing a high point in Ancient Egyptian art, sculpture, and jewelry. Senusret consolidated many of his father's policies: maintaining a military presence coupled with trading links in the south, building a line of forts which extended to the Second Cataract of the Nile. Quarries and mines were exploited throughout the country for stone and gold. He also led expeditions to the south and for the first time to the desert oases. These are recorded on stelae left there. His overall control is documented at almost three dozen sites, from Alexandria to Aswan.

Senusret rebuilt the temple to Ra-Atum at the ancient sun city of Heliopolis, erecting two giant red granite obelisks, one of which survives as the oldest standing obelisk in Egypt.

Senusret acknowledged his son Amenemhat II as co-ruler some years before his death, the young prince following in his footsteps by campaigning in the south. Senusret finished his pyramid at Lisht, a mile south of his father, Amenemhat I's, and — as with his father's pyramid — the burial chamber is inaccessible due to ground water. Nine smaller satellite pyramids belonging to his royal ladies are also enclosed in the complex. An exquisite kiosk belonging to him was found filling a later pylon of the Eighteenth Dynasty at Karnak and has been rebuilt.

AMENEMHAT II

1922–1878BC

Also known as Nubkaura, Amenemhat II succeeded to the throne following the death of his father; he then reigned for another 34 years.

During his reign the Faiyum was developed and the Bahr Yusef, the branch of the Nile linking the Faiyum to the Nile proper, was enlarged and deepened. He strove to continue the policies of his father and grandfather and, because of their previous hard work, things were more settled and the country consequently more prosperous.

Egyptian expeditions were also made to the Red Sea and the land of Punt; there was contact with Crete and an increase in immigration of Levantines into the country. Amenemhat built his pyramid at Dashur to the east of the Fourth Dynasty pyramids of Snefru.

SENUSRET II

1880–1874BC

Also known as Sesostris II and Khakheperra, Senusret had the usual co-regency with his father, which by this time had become tradition for

Statue of Senusret III. He was a brave pharaoh who re-shaped Egyptian domestic and foreign policy, by reducing the power of the local nomarchs and creating three vizierates to manage the country's internal affairs. At the same time he resumed regular foreign campaigns to stifle the various threats coming from south, east, and westerly directions. His pyramid was built at Dashur.

this dynasty. It lasted for at least three years before his father passed on and he inherited the throne. He was secure in his legacy and his reign was peaceful.

Senusret continued with the expansion and development of the Faiyum and profited greatly from Egypt's possessions in Palestine, the Sinai, and Nubia. He also made sure he had cordial relationships with the provincial nobility.

Senusret built his pyramid at Lahun, and as with all Middle Kingdom pyramids, it had a mud-brick core, faced with white limestone. In an effort to outwit the tomb-robbers, the entrance to the pyramid was hidden in the paving surrounding the edifice, but to no avail. Once the casing had been robbed, the core fell quickly into ruin. Nearby the pyramid the Egyptologist Petrie found a town built to house the workmen who built the king's funerary complex, excavations of which have yielded much information on Ancient Egyptian daily life.

Senusret III

1874–1855BC

Also known as Sesostris III and Khakaura, Senruset III succeeded to the throne and is thought to have reigned for about 37 years.

Manetho describes him as a great warrior with a huge physique. He was successful in containing the nomarchs whose power was once again on the rise. He created a new system of government dividing the country into three administrative departments: North, South, and Head of the South and Lower Nubia, each with a vizier. His own strong centralized control manifested in his court, to which the provincial nobles were drawn.

Once Senusret III had the country stabilized he concentrated on foreign policy. The previous two reigns had been comparatively peaceful with the inevitable rise of nomad action on the borders. Senusret took military action against various tribes enabling the frontier to be set at Semna, with more forts built to hold the new ground.

He next began by rebuilding and expanding the canal around the First Cataract (originally built in the time of the Old Kingdom) and then carried out various campaigns against the Nubians, leaving commemorative stelae recording his exploits behind him, warning future generations to make the same amount of effort. In fact he pushed Egypt's boundary further south than ever before and seems to have led a campaign into Palestine as well. Much of the wealth and booty gained in these campaigns went in tribute to the temples in Egypt, especially to that of Amun at Thebes.

Senusret III built his pyramid at Dashur, at the southern end of the Memphite necropolis. It was the largest of the Twelfth Dynasty, but, again, all that remains is the rubble mound of its mudbrick core; once the limestone casing had been stolen none of the Middle Kingdom pyramids could survive.

As time went on, different methods were tried to hide the entrances but the robbers always found a way to break in. Senusret's spectacular white limestone-lined burial chamber was found empty. However, some fine jewelry was found in the satellite shaft tombs of his wives and his sister. Among other of his constructions was a temple to Montu, the Theban war god, at Medamud.

Amenemhat III

1855–1808BC

Also known as Nimaatra, Amenemhat III was the eldest son of Senusret III, who came to the throne after the usual co-regency. His reign was the peak of Twelfth Dynasty power and prestige as the achievements of his forbears, especially his father, enabled him to exploit the resources of the conquered areas of Nubia and Syria. Internally, the Faiyum was still further developed, the massive irrigation project begun by his father was completed, and a huge temple to the local god Sobek was built there. Amenemhat also exploited the country's quarries and the turquoise mines of the Sinai.

Unusually for the Middle Kingdom, Amenemhat built two pyramids for himself, one at Dashur, the other at Hawara. The first was probably abandoned because it cracked during construction and the king was finally buried in the Hawaran pyramid. This contained an almost clichéd number of traps and counter-measures in an attempt to confound thieves. The burial chamber itself was carved out of a single giant block of quartzite and all the shafts were sealed and back-filled — all to no avail.

Amenemhet IV

1808–1799BC

Also known as Maakherura, Amenemhat IV was the son of Amenemhat III and the last male ruler of the Twelfth Dynasty. Little is known about this king, as his reign was fairly short and not many records belonging to his time survive. There are various inscriptions in Syria and also Nubia (or Greater Egypt) down to the Third Cataract. It is also known that he completed his father's temple projects in the Faiyum. No definite pyramid has yet been assigned to him, but it is thought that two ruined pyramids some five miles to the south of Dashur could be those of Amenemhat IV and his successor, Queen Sobeknefru.

Queen Sobeknefru

1799–1795BC

Also known as Sobekkara, she was sister and possibly wife of Amenemhat IV. Whichever, she was close enough to inherit the throne on his death. Sobeknefru is the first positively proven queen in Ancient Egyptian history; while, perhaps the earlier Queen Nitocret was more than legend, there is, as yet, no hard evidence to support this. Not a great deal is known of Sobeknefru at the end of the dynasty, as very little in the way of written records have survived. Her reign seems to have been very short: she completed the construction of her brother's mortuary temple at Hawara, known in later ancient times as the labyrinth because of its complexity.

Again there is no hard evidence as yet of the location of her tomb. It is possible that one of the two unnamed pyramids at Mazghuna, south of Dashur, might belong to her.

Osiris was thought to be buried in the ancient necropolis at Abydos.

THIRTEENTH DYNASTY 1795–AFTER 1650BC

The changeover to the Thirteenth Dynasty seems to have been smooth enough, despite a queen predecessor, but the difference between the two regimes is marked. Instead of a handful of long-serving monarchs there are unknown numbers of kings listed for this dynasty, having a total span of some 70 years — a high turnover that left little in the way of records and many unfinished pyramid complexes. They still ruled from the previous dynasty's fortress city Itj-tawy, near the Faiyum, and central government was maintained for most of the dynasty, though there are comparatively few monuments attributed to the pharaohs, so their true chronology and order is in question.

The kings of the Thirteenth Dynasty were not all from the same royal line, but consisted of various commoners and military men — men of the moment needed for their strength of purpose. The unfinished remains of a number of pyramid complexes belonging to this dynasty lie at South Saqqara and also at Dashur. Their internal complexity increases with each structure, as vain attempts were made to thwart the inevitable tomb robbers. Other of this dynasty's kings had time only for the most simple of shaft burials, their reigns so brief that nothing is known about them.

WEGAF

Also known as Khutawyra, the dynasty begins with King Wegaf, who seems to have ruled for no more than three or four years. Almost the only evidence of this king are four boundary stelae marking out an area in the ancient necropolis of Abydos, which contemporaries thought to include the grave of the great god Osiris.

AMENY INTEF IV

Apart from one inscription and a mention in various king lists there is no further information or evidence for this king, other than that he was probably also known as Sankhibra.

HOR

Also known as Awibra, Hor's tomb has been found next to that of Amenemhat III at Dashur and, being so insignificant, it was only partially robbed, leaving possibly the fullest collection of Middle Kingdom funerary equipment discovered thus far, including an impressive wooden *Ka* statue of the king. The Canon of Turin papyrus confirms that Hor's reign was very short.

SOBEKHOTEP III

Also called Sekhemrasewadjtawy, he was the son of a Theban prince named Montjuhotpe and his wife the Lady Iuhetibu. In contrast to the kings preceding him, some of whom may even have seized power and about whom nothing is known, there is more archaeological evidence to support the existence of Sobekhotep III, although there were up to eight Sobekhoteps in this dynasty, not all of whom anything is known about. Sobekhotep had various children — at least two daughters and two sons, none of whom followed him to the throne.

Bronze statuette of Neferhotep I. Ruling from Itj-tawy, near the Faiyum, the Thirteenth Dynasty left comparatively little physical evidence due to its rapid turnover of kings.

KHENDJER

Also called Userkara. At Saqqara there are four mud-brick pyramid remains attributed to kings of this dynasty, with one at least being positively identified as belonging to Khendjer, though no body was found. He is also known to have renovated and adorned the tomb of the First Dynasty's King Djer at Abydos, which was by then believed to be the tomb of the god Osiris.

SOBEKHOTEP IV

c.1726BC

The period from the reign of Sobekhotep IV — also known as Khaneferra — and his brothers, Neferhotep I and Sihator, seems to have been the most stable of this dynasty, one of the rare occasions when there was some blood relationship between successors to the throne. There are a number of colossal statues of the king that have survived as well as a few ruined and fragmentary temple reliefs. He is also known to have campaigned in Nubia, where stelae record his achievements.

NEFERHOTEP I

Also called Khasekhemra, he was the brother of Sobekhotep IV. There is a relief at Byblos of Neferhotep I receiving homage from the local princes, as well as other evidence of him in Nubia, proving that, despite the fragmentary evidence and fast turnover, there was still considerable substance to this dynasty. It took a time for them gradually to lose grip on what had been bequeathed to them by their predecessors. Neferhotep I is supposed to have reigned for at least a decade and to have been succeeded briefly by his son or brother Sihator, about whom virtually nothing is known. He also maintained this dynasty's interest in the tomb thought to belong to Osiris at Abydos.

Right: The vulture was a manifestation of the goddess Nekhbet, the protective goddess of southern Egypt.

At the same time as the kings of the elusive and mysterious Fourteenth Dynasty were ruling their patch, a series of Semitic kings was beginning to take control of another part of the delta, at its eastern edge. These rulers became known as the Hyksos (Desert princes). They were initially foreigners who had been infiltrating the delta region for many years, who adopted many of the Egyptian ways, including their titles for their monarchs. They introduced some new gods, but adopted the Ancient Egyptian ones too, unusually electing Set as their main god, probably because he paralleled some desert god of their own. This was later to make Set anathema to the Egyptians, who, after expelling the Hyksos, systematically destroyed all trace of them, leaving few primary sources.

As the settlers gradually infiltrated the delta, they became wealthier and more established, slowly spreading out from their stronghold at Avaris. The five or six main Hyksos rulers identified by Manetho are allocated a span of 108 years. The badly damaged Turin papyrus gives only a certain amount of information that obviously cannot be complete. The Hyksos were responsible for the introduction of horses and chariots into the technology of Egyptian warfare, along with improvements in arms and armor. They sacked Memphis in about 1720BC, but preferred to remain in their eastern strongholds, where they then co-existed quite amicably with the emerging Theban Seventeenth Dynasty, but only until it was strong enough to launch a purge of the Hyksos and reunify the country. The remains of the Hyksos cities reveal a systematic destruction that was obviously completed with a passionate hatred and determination.

Ruling from the eastern delta area concurrent with the final years of the Thirteenth Dynasty, the Fourteenth Dynasty represents the gradual breakdown of centralized control that would eventually lead to the beginning of the Second Intermediate Period. Manetho states that it lasted for some 57 years, but the number and names of this dynasty's kings are not known. In fact virtually nothing is known about them, as the moist delta region has left much less in the way of archaeological evidence to decipher than the more arid south.

At this time too Nubia managed to break away from Egyptian domination. It would eventually become an ally of the delta kings in their fight against the Thebans.

FIFTEENTH DYNASTY 1650-1550BC HYKSOS

SHESHI
Also known as Salitis and Mayebra, the earliest known Hyksos king.

YAKUBHER
Also known as Meruserra.

KHYAN
Also called Seuserenra.

APEPI I
Also known as Apophis and Auserra.

APEPI II
Also known as Aqenra.

SIXTEENTH DYNASTY 1650-1550BC EASTERN DELTA

Operating out of the delta, almost certainly under the shadow and with the complicity of the Hyksos, only two names are known for the Sixteenth Dynasty pharaohs. These are deciphered from commemorative scarabs, and their names do not appear in cartouches. These pharaohs were obviously associated with Byblos and southern Palestine.

ANATHER

YAKOBAAM

SEVENTEENTH DYNASTY 1650-1550BC THEBAN

While the Hyksos ruled along with their underkings in the delta, the Seventeenth Dynasty was gradually evolving at Thebes. They ruled over an area from Elephantine to Abydos, preserving the old traditional ways. Both sides seemed content to allow the existence of the other without too much fuss, but the Thebans were merely biding their time. Gradually, as they became more confident in their power, they began to arm themselves and rise against the Hyksos, beginning a campaign that would finally see the Hyksos expelled from the delta and wiped as thoroughly as possible from Egyptian history.

Many of the Seventeenth Dynasty kings were known as Intef, an old Theban royal name that had much resonance. Their huge heavy coffins, decorated with vulture-wings and known as *rishi*, have been found on the west bank of Thebes, in poor quality tombs cut into the hillside along with the remains of steep mud brick pyramids. There seem to have been almost 20 kings in this dynasty about whom little is known until the kings Tao I and II, who began to gain ground in the struggle against the Hyksos.

SOBEKEMSAF II
Also known as Sekhemra Shedtawy. Sobekemsaf's tomb remained intact

until the Twentieth Dynasty when the robbers were caught and tried in the reign of Ramesses IX. The trial details the break-in by some of the very workers who built such monuments.

INTEF VII

Also known as Nubkheperra, Intef VII was the successor to Sobekemsaf II. However, the only hard evidence for this king is his coffin.

TAO I

Also known as Taa I and Sanakhtenra. There is very little real information about this king. His wife Tetisheri, the mother of his successor Tao II, seems to have been a powerful and influential woman. She outlived her husband and her grandson Ahmose I built a cenotaph tomb for her close to his own. Later she was seen as being an important ancestor of the Eighteenth Dynasty.

TAO II

c.1560BC

Also known as Taa II and Seqenra. Surnamed "Qen" — "The Brave."

It seems highly probable that Tao II was actually killed on the battlefield in the war of liberation against the Hyksos, which conflict greatly intensified during his reign. His original tomb has never been discovered, but his body from the Royal Cache at Deir-el-Bahari, bears the terrible scars of full battle. It was he who opened up a new campaign against the Hyksos of the delta, a task which his son, Ahmose I, the first king of the Eighteenth Dynasty, would complete.

It is Tao Seqenra who features in the Ramessid folk tale about a quarrel that broke out between himself and the Hyksos king, Apepi I, at Avaris, complaining that the hippopotami of Thebes were disturbing his sleep!

Tao II was buried below a rather small pyramid in the Theban necropolis, before being removed to the Royal Cache at Deir el-Bahari.

KAMOSE

c.1550BC

Also known as Wadjkheperra, Kamose was either an elder son of Tao II, who inherited the throne from his father, or a younger brother. Following the death of Tao Seqenra there was a lull in the fighting, but with the crowning of Kamose the Thebans launched their final victorious campaign, which would result in the expulsion of the Hyksos from the delta. Kamose fought his way across the country, intercepting on his way a messenger bound for Nubia with the request of diversionary attacks on Kamose's rear. He was able to take precautions against such an eventuality and went on to push the Hyksos into their capital of Avaris, shutting them up in the eastern delta. Though victorious, his reign was brief, and he died before the start of the next fighting season. He was buried at Thebes in a simple *rishi* coffin.

Above: Hathor was lady guardian of the western lands of the dead, protectress of the necropoli, and of the dead.

Below: The temple is set in a series of terraces that reach into the cliffs at Deir el-Bahari. It is a stunning and distinctive architectural masterpiece that drew inspiration from the similar — though now destroyed — complex of Nebhetepra Mentuhotep II nearby.

THE NEW KINGDOM 1550–1069BC

EIGHTEENTH DYNASTY 1550-1295BC

The Eighteenth Dynasty saw the beginning of the New Kingdom, which would soon become the final great flowering of Ancient Egyptian civilization and culture. These newly emergent native rulers would no longer live in isolation along their desert-protected river, but rather would carve out increased safety buffers that would constitute an empire, set within a great interaction of peoples and countries that had now linked up to make the ancient world of the Mediterranean and the Middle East. This burst of brilliance, powered by advances and influences that came from outside, would have at its roots and bring about results that were still quintessentially Egyptian. This period would also see warrior kings such as Thutmose III and Ramesses II and III, the heretic and opulent Amarna Interlude of Akhenaten and even a queen of iron will and great talent, Hatshepsut.

Ahmose I

1550–1295BC

Also known as Amosis I and Nebpehtyra, he was the son of Tao Seqenra and, perhaps, a brother or nephew of Kamose, both lost in the war against the Hyksos. It fell to Ahmose to finally rid the land of the

Another view of the mortuary temple complex at Deir el-Bahari, with a close up of the Hathor-headed pillars at the shrine of Hathor on the second terrace. The mortuary temple was used in later years as a Coptic monastery, which gave the area its name.

shepherd kings and once again consolidate the borders. He seems to have come to the throne at quite an early age and, as a result, did not continue the war straight away. In fact, in the first decade of his reign the Hyksos managed to regain territory as far as Heliopolis, as Ahmose's operations began again with the taking of this city. Finally, he besieged Avaris for a considerable length of time. When it fell at last, he carried out mopping-up operations throughout the delta, followed by a series of rapid campaigns in Syria culminating in the destruction of the Palestinian fortress of Sharuhen. With this the final expulsion of the Hyksos was complete and he could turn his attention southwards to Nubia. Here he regained territory up to the Second Cataract, establishing a new administration with a viceroy at its head. The first one is known to have been called Djehuty.

During this time, when Ahmose was kept busy re-establishing Egypt's sovereignty, there were occasional uprisings in the delta area originally settled by the Hyksos. It seems that Ahmose could depend on the queen-mother Ahtope to take care of these disturbances. Stelae acknowledging his debt have been found and her mummy had Egypt's highest military award (the Gold Flies) upon it.

Ahmose had so much to do that he inevitably had to delegate power more to the nomarchs, with many gifts of land, and important positions at court and within the administration. He also began to rebuild, initiating various temple building projects, testified at Abydos. Manetho gives his reign as being 25-26 years long.

He married his sister, Ahmose-Nefertiri, and had a number of children, amongst whom was his original heir, Amosis-Ankh, and his eventual successor, Amenhotep I. He was buried somewhere in the Theban necropolis — his tomb has so far not been discovered — and he had a cenotaph at Abydos. His well-preserved mummy was eventually found in the great Royal Cache of 1881.

Amenhotep I

1525–1504BC

Also called Djeserkara, Amenhotep I succeeded his father to the throne at a young age, so his mother, Ahmose-Nefertiri, might have been regent for a while. He ruled for about 20 years, in which time he led at least one campaign into Nubia, continuing his father's work of pacification. He also undertook various building projects including additions to the temple of Amun at Karnak.

He seems to have been the first king to site his mortuary temple away from his tomb, which has never been positively identified. His mummy was found along with his father's in the great Royal Cache.

Thutmose I

1504–1492BC

He was also known as Tuthmosis I and Akheperkara. Although his reign was short — he a middle-aged military man when he came to the throne — Thutmose I was a warrior-tactician of great talent, who campaigned extensively, pushing the borders of Egypt further into Nubia and Palestine. He legitimized his claim to the throne through his marriage to the daughter of Ahmose I. His short reign was packed full of action, with a series of brilliant campaigns that ensured the survival of the Eighteenth Dynasty and set Ancient Egypt on the road to empire. In Nubia he expanded Egyptian sovereignty beyond the Fourth Cataract. In the Sinai he seems even to have crossed the Euphrates in a campaign against the Mitanni.

Thutmose I also extensively remodelled the great temple at Karnak, in honor of Amun for granting him success and victory in his military campaigns. Here was another rise in the power and kudos of Amun — and his priesthood. Two sons predeceased him, leaving his third son, Mutneferu by another wife (Mutnofret) to inherit as Thutmose II.

Thutmose II

1492–1479BC

Also known as Tuthmosis II and Akheperenra, Thutmose II suddenly inherited the throne at a young age on the death of his father. He was married to the daughter of his father and Queen Ahmose (she was called Hatshepsut), a strong woman who would eventually make her own bid for the throne. He reigned for about 14 years, before dying in his early thirties. He suffered from poor health, but this did not stop him prosecuting successful campaigns in Nubia and then Syria. He had no sons with Hatshepsut but had one son from another minor wife (Iset), who was also named Thutmose. When Thutmose II died his son inherited the throne at too young an age and consequently his aunt Hatshepsut became regent.

Queen Hatshepsut

1473–1458BC

For the first seven years of Thutmose III's reign, Hatshepsut (also called Maatkara) did not step beyond the bounds of protocol. She was regent, appearing with queenly attributes, but by the seventh year she felt she had built up enough support from her officials and had herself declared king. She took royal titles in cartouches and was portrayed as a male monarch, though she continued to date from Thutmose III's regnal years and included him on her monuments. She played a cunning game of dual-kingship, constantly attempting to legitimize her position with propaganda.

Queen Hatshepsut next began to build herself a unique and magnificent mortuary temple in the bay of the cliffs at Deir el-Bahari. B uilt largely from limestone, it rose in three broad colonnaded terraces to a central rock-cut sanctuary. The temple was built under the supervision of Senenmut, a steward of the queen's who rose to the highest offices under her patronage.

The main temple was dedicated to Amun but there were subsidiary ones to both Hathor and Anubis on the second terrace. It also features a "birth relief" — a propaganda wall which shows Amun visiting Hatshepsut's mother, implying her own divine conception. She was also portrayed with the insignia of kingship and used her father's reputation to bolster her claim. It was all nonsense and political expediency.

During this time it seems that

A statue of the only true female pharaoh, Hatshepsut, builder of the famous Deir el-Bahari temple complex. Though portrayed by necessity as male, the face has a softer more feminine shape and profile.

Thutmose III (the rightful king, but king only in name) was reduced to junior co-regent and tasked with the more physically demanding civil and military expeditions. Hatshepsut continued adding to the temple to Amun at Thebes, but also set about restoring other temples that had fallen into disrepair or suffered during the war with the Hyksos.

Her first tomb, which was never used but cut when she was queen regnant with Thutmose II, was in the Valley of the Kings, but she cut another at the foot of the cliffs in the same valley. The original intention was to burrow under the cliffs to her temple on the other side, but the tunnel collapsed. She then took over the tomb of her father, Thutmose I, enlarging it to accommodate herself alongside him. (Thutmose III would eventually reinter his grandfather in another, separate tomb). Some 22 years after the death of her husband, Thutmose II, Hatshepsut's reign ended in mystery — she just drops out of history completely. It was a good while after this, perhaps as much as two decades later, that her monuments were defaced, which only makes her disappearance more mysterious. In the future her reign was seen as anathema and she was not included in the king lists.

Tuthmosis III

1479–1425BC

With Hatsheput's death, Thutmose III — also known as Menkheperra —

Right: Wall relief depicting Pharaoh Thutmose III. Seen in the classic pose of the "smiting icon," the king holds up the hair of his vanquished enemy while at the same time delivering the death-blow with the royal mace. Such a scene was a standard format used over the millenia by almost every pharaoh down to and including the Roman emperors. Its intention was to show the personal strength and invincibility of the monarch, that even in battle he was god-like.

came into his inheritance. Senenmut, her powerful minister, had died the year before and could no longer stand in his way. Perhaps Thutmose even had a hand in her demise, for he certainly hated her, and eventually set about defacing any inscriptions and obliterating her from history, including various damage to her mortuary temple and to the tombs of her courtiers.

At Deir el-Bahari, tucked between Mentuhotep and Hatshepsut's temples, Thutmose III built one of his own, which seems to have been destroyed soon after construction by a rockfall from the high cliffs behind it. Nearby he also built a rock-cut shrine dedicated to Hathor.

Tuthmosis III started off his military campaigns in the second year of his solo reign, aiming eastwards. An account of it was inscribed on the inside walls at Karnak to the greater glory of the king and the god Amun. Thutmose soon revealed his tactical genius for war. In less than five months he traveled from Thebes all along the Syrian coast, fighting decisive battles and capturing over 350 cities, establishing an Egyptian hegemony and peace that would last a hundred years — no mean achievement at this busy crossroads of competing cultures. He also mounted punitive raids into Nubia.

The 17 campaigns into Asia were the bequest of Thutmose III, and it is not for nothing he was called the Napoleon of Ancient Egypt. He also repaired once again the old canal past the First Cataract, building temples, and leaving commemorative stelae in his wake. Many temples were enriched by the spoils from these successful ventures, and none more so than the great temple at Karnak as he gave back to the god for supplying victory. Thus the problem of an over-powerful Karnak priesthood — which would culminate in priest-kings — steadily grew in momentum. Foreign princes were brought back to Egypt as hostage for good behavior, still further spreading Egyptian influence on their return home.

Thutmose III's reign was noted for its magnificent and opulent artwork, the superb quality of tombs and carvings, and the general high standard of all his construction work, as well as his military exploits and conquests. When he died in about 1450BC he was buried in his tomb in the Valley of the Kings, but his mummy was found in the great Royal Cache at Deir el-Bahari.

Amenhotep II

1427–1400BC

Also known as Amenophis II and Aakheperura, Amenhotep II was born in Memphis, the son of

Below: Stone statue of a seated Amenhotep II. The seventh ruler of the Eighteenth Dynasty, whose long reign saw the loss of Egyptian possessions in Syria and Palestine, and the beginning of the rise of the Hittites.

Right: The famous Colossi of Memnon. See overleaf for details.

Thutmose III and his wife Hatshepsut-Meritra. Slim and athletic like his forbears, Amenhotep II also did well on the battlefield, having to exert himself almost immediately when, on the death of his father, some of the Asiatic cities rose in revolt against Egyptian rule. Amenhotep wasted no time moving swiftly overland into northern Palestine, fought his way across the Orontes and returned laden with princely prisoners and booty with which to still further enrich the Great Temple of Amun. In his third regnal year Nubia was the target, where he completed the temples begun by his father at Elephantine and Amada. In the nionth year of his reign he was back in Palestine again.

After this initial military burst proving things had not changed, he settled down to a peaceful reign. He built extensively at Thebes and was eventually buried in the Valley of the Kings, which was where he was found, battered but intact. His tomb had been plundered in ancient times and then later was used as a cache for other royal mummies, containing apart from himself: Thutmose IV, Amenhotep III, Merenptah, Seti II, Siptah, Ramesses IV, V, and VI, three women (one of whom is possibly Queen Ti), and a young unknown boy.

Thutmose IV

1400–1390BC

Also known as Tuthmosis IV and Menkheperura, Thutmose IV was a minor son of Amenhotep II, the father of Amenhotep III, and the grandfather of Akhenaten. The Dream Stele between the paws of the Giza Sphinx (which tells of his dream promising kingship if he cleared away the sand surrounding Horus on the Horizon) seems to indicate that he was not first in line to inherit the throne. It is obvious legitimizing propaganda.

No great military campaigns were recorded during his reign, although in the south there was an expedition early on into Nubia. In fact his foreign policy inaugurated a period of reconciliation in the east, with a marriage to a princess of the Mitanni. It is from this king's reign that are dated some of the best known and most lavishly decorated private tombs at Thebes which belong to the nobility. Thutmose himself was buried in the Valley of the Kings, his tomb being robbed in ancient times. His mummy was found hidden in the tomb of Amenhotep II.

Left and Previous Page: The famous Colossi of Memnon. In fact these two giant seated statues are all that remains of the huge mortuary temple of Amenhotep III. This king's reign saw the architectural and artistic achievements of the Eighteenth Dynasty continue in their quality and brilliance, along with the beginnings of the rise in importance of Aten.

Amenhotep III

1390–1352BC

Also known as Amenophis III and Nubmaatra, Amenhotep III had a long reign of almost 40 years, one of the most prosperous and stable in Ancient Egyptian history. Thutmose III had laid the foundations for such peace and prosperity of empire with his masterful strategic campaigns in Syria, Nubia, and Libya. Thus almost no military activity was necessary in the reigns of Thutmose IV and Amenhotep III.

Amenhotep was the son of Thutmose IV by one of his chief wives, Mutemwiya, daughter of the Mitannian king. He himself had a big harem and several of his wives were also diplomatic marriages to foreign princesses, but his chief wife was Tiy, whom he married before coming to the throne. She was not of noble birth, but came from an important military family in the delta. Amenhotep went against tradition in her representations, which were equal in size to his.

There was some minor military activity at the beginning of his reign — the usual establishing of perimeters — then a reign of opulence and richness, as evinced in the buildings and tombs. This dynasty had untold wealth as the Egyptian empire reached its maximum size and tribute poured in from numerous conquests. A series of strong warrior-kings had carved out Egypt's hegemony against all comers. But the eastern opposition was of a different caliber to the primitive tribes of the Nubian and Libyan deserts, although they, too, were influenced by the jewel on their doorstep.

The last decades of Amenhotep's reign saw many new buildings, artworks, and new heights of luxury at court as the wealth and tribute of the empire continued to arrive. A lasting proof of this are the innumerable commemorative scarabs left from his reign. The Great Temple of Amun was massively furnished and provided for, reaching dizzying heights of wealth and prestige as the kingdom's premier spiritual power center. There was also a new temple dedicated to Amun at Luxor. However, despite all this wealth, the famous Colossi of Memmnon are all that remains of Amenhotep's mortuary temple.

Amenhotep's robbed tomb in the Valley of the Kings was found to have originally been prepared for Thutmose IV. His main wife, Tiy, survived him by several years, perhaps as much as a decade as there are references to her in some of the Amarna tombs and it is known she lived at Akhenaten's capital of Akhetaten.

Akhenaten

1352–1336BC

Originally called Amenhotep IV, and also Amenophis IV or Neferkheperurawaenra, he changed his name early on in his reign (the fifth year) to Akhenaten, spearheading his own politico-religious revolution. Modern Amarna was Akhetaten, his new capital city, whose traces have finally revealed the existence of a reign that later generations abominated and expunged from their history.

Was Akhenaten's a daring attempt

to counteract the growing power of the Great Temple of Amun-Ra and its priesthood, or the final manifestation of a patently unstable egoist, or even both? Perhaps he served a co-regency with his father — traces of the later Amarna style have been recognized in some art towards the end of Amenhotep III's reign.

Akhenaten was crowned at Karnak. Like his father he married an astonishingly beautiful commoner, Nefertiti, daughter of the Vizier Ay. Was Akhenaten more of a philosopher than his predecessors or did he merely reap the benefits of their empire making, unconcerned with the practical day-to-day effort of maintaining his inheritance? His reign poses many unanswered questions.

Amenhotep III had already been

Left: Red quartzite head of Akhenaten. Akhenaten's reign ushered in changes in the arts of painting and literature, sculpture, and building that would become known to Egyptologists as the Amarna Interlude.

Above: A small sculpted portrait of Akhenaten, the pharaoh who encouraged his artists to represent what they saw.

Right: Famous bust of Akhenaten's principal queen, Nefertiti. She bore the king six daughters who featured often in the temple and palace reliefs of the new capital city, Akhetaten.

aware of the threat from Amun's priesthood and attempted to curb it; Akhenaten would go much further, trying to establish a monotheistic cult to the Aten — a manifestation of the sun as a disk. There was some family patronage of this aspect of the god already evident, but now Aten became accessible only through Akhenaten himself, so making the priesthood unnecessary.

Akhenaten began by building a temple to the Aten near the temple of Amun at Karnak, initially proscribing the cult of Amun and then in time extending the ban on to all the other gods. In Year Six of his reign he relocated to virgin ground midway between Memphis and Thebes, today known as el-Amarna. The hymn to the Aten is recorded to its fullest extent in the tomb of his vizier, Ay. Akhenaten himself is credited with its composition. Needless to say it was only his court who followed his precedent, for this was not a religion that would appeal to the Egyptian people at large. Even at Amarna the old ways continued. Dismantling the old priesthood must have had consequences, but by and large the state religion did not have as much to do with the people anyway.

Akhenaten was interested in art and truth, not policy, leaving the administration of the country to his civil and military services. This neglect and in-turning was to have repercussions for the empire: the civil and military spheres came under the control of two strong figures, Ay and Horembeb, who sealed their alliance and joined the king's family through the latter's marriage to another daughter of Ay, Mutnodjme, sister of Nefertiti. Ay and Horembeb kept things running as smoothly as they could, while Akhenaten pursued his own agenda.

His chief sculptor and master of works, Bek, records that the king instructed them to paint true to life. Such realism was a radical departure from the traditional royal iconography. The court followed the unusual and radical royal art protocol, being portrayed in an elongated and heightened, feminine, curvy fashion. His queen, Nefertiti, featured much more prominently than was usual, at least up until the twelfth year of Akhenaten's reign, when she disappears, probably dying and being buried in the royal tomb at Akhetaten. Her daughter, Merytaten, succeeded her as Akhenaten's main wife.

Akhenaten died around 1334BC, sometime during his sixteenth regnal year. His body has never been found — almost certainly it was destroyed and he was not to be mentioned in future King Lists.

SMENKHKARA

1338–1336BC

Also called Nefernefruaten and Ankhkheperura, Smenkhara was Akhenaten's heir, and possibly his younger brother or son. His reign was very short — probably only a two-year co-regency. He married Merytaten, senior heiress of the royal line. It seems that Smenkhara was definitely "old school" when it came to religion and even when he was heir to the throne he was already manifesting a return to orthodoxy. But he died a few months before Akhenaten, who had him consequently buried in Atenist fashion. It was not until after Akhenaten's own death that Smenkhkara was removed from the Atenist Amarna burial ground and reinterred in the Valley of the Kings, probably concurrent with Tutankhamun. Smenkhkara, like his father and brother, was omitted from later king lists.

TUTANKHAMUN

1336–1327BC

Until the fantastic discovery of his virtually intact tomb, very little was known about Tutankhamun — also called Nebkheperura — for he, too, was omitted from the later king lists. From things found in his tomb it is known that he spent some time at Akhetaten, along with the rest of the court. At that time he was known as Tutankhaten, and was still so named when he was crowned at Memphis. He inherited age nine and, with virtually no family left, was probably under the care of the vizier Ay, and the general Horembeb, who implemented policy in his name. His mother was perhaps Queen Kiya, a junior queen of Akhenaten's, who came to prominence after the death of Nefertiti.

Tutankhamun was married to Ankhesenpaten, his older half-sister. Within two years of his coronation Tutankhaten and his queen had changed their Aten names to Amun, signaling a return to the old orthodoxy. Temples were reopened and restored, and new work undertaken at Karnak and Luxor, although the credit for all these things was later assumed by Horembeb.

Also during the young king's reign, various military campaigns were launched into Nubia and Syria, which reflect perhaps attempts to maintain the empire and recover the ground lost under Akhenaten's neglect. There must have been much general relief that the old ways were being reasserted.

Tutankhamun died young, in about his 17th year. The exact cause of death is not known, perhaps an unforeseen accident carried him off — the size of his tomb and some of the objects in it seem to infer this. His death must have raised a question about the succession for it is known that Ankhesenamun wrote to the Hittite king Suppiluliumas asking to marry one of his sons. Suppiluliumas

The famous golden funeral mask of Tutankhamun. Until Carter's discovery of his virtually intact tomb, almost nothing was known about this boy-king. He was born in the Amarna period and distanced himself from the Aten heresy by changing his name from Tutankhaten soon after inheriting the throne.

Small statuette of Tutankhamun from his tomb in the Valley of the Kings. He is wearing the deshret, the Red Crown of Lower Egypt.

sent prince Zannanza, who got no further than the border, where he was promptly murdered.

AY

1327–1323BC

On the death of Tutankhamun, Ay — also known as Kheperkheperura — who had been the vizier of the previous two reigns, now seized his chance. To validate his claim to the throne, he married Ankhesenamun, Tutankhamun's wife, one of the daughters of Akhenaten. Like many of his recent predecessors Ay's reign was short, with little to show in the way of building and monuments (those few he built were usurped by Horembeb), and his tomb in the western valley was thoroughly smashed up, with his cartouches hacked off.

His mortuary temple was at Medinet Habu.

HOREMBEB

1323–1295BC

Also known as Djeserkheperura, Horembeb was an ambitious commoner, hailing from Herakleopolis, whose meteoric military career eventually enabled him to seize the throne. He first served under Amenhotep III, becoming commander-in-chief of the army in the reign of Akhenaten. Perhaps he was also a power behind the throne during the reign of Tutankhamun (along with Ay). Certainly there was a general return to orthodoxy in religious and political matters, and given the weakness of the royal line, it was inevitable that a strong man could prevail.

Horembeb, already middle-aged, declared himself king in 1321, strengthening his claim to the throne through his marriage to Nefertiti's sister, Mutnodjme. He masterminded the continued return to the old ways, restoring the priesthood of Amun and reopening the temples. Perhaps learning from his own rapid advancement he safeguarded himself by dividing the army into two separate (southern and northern) commands. He took over the monuments of his predecessors, Ay and Tutankhamun, and initiated works at the great temple of Amun at Karnak, destroying all he could of Akhetaten and its creator in the process. He took over Ay's mortuary temple at Medinet Habu and dated his reign from the death of Amenhotep III, thus expunging the Amarna interlude altogether.

His unused tomb at Saqqara was filled with high quality carvings representing his life and achievements, but he was buried in the Valley of the Kings where a tomb containing his sarcophagus and other wooden statues of him were found. His mummy has never been found.

NINETEENTH DYNASTY 1295-1186BC

RAMESSES I
(1295-1294BC)
Also called Menpehtyra, Ramesses I was the vizier and close friend of Horembeb, and came from a similar military background — he was a professional soldier the son of a troop commander named Seti and his family originated from Avaris, the old Hyksos capital in the delta. The previous pharaoh, Horembeb, was childless, so he passed the succession on to his friend, who came to the throne in middle age, for a brief reign of about two years. He still had time to build two temples, at Abydos and Buhen. He also completed the Second Pylon at Karnak. His tomb in the Valley of the Kings is small and unfinished, and his mummy has never been found. His wife, Sitra, was not buried in his tomb but set a precedent by being the first to be buried in the Valley of the Queens at Thebes.

Left and Overleaf: Three views of the Valley of the Kings. Following the defeat of the Hyksos, the Theban rulers of the New Kingdom Eighteenth Dynasty began to build tombs that befitted the kings of an Egypt once again united. The pyramids had proved vulnerable, so, beginning with Thutmose I, the tombs of the pharaohs were carved out of a desolate valley in the arid Theban Hills.

Left: In the Valley of the Kings lie tunnel tombs which led down to subterranean halls and burial chambers covered with painted texts and carved reliefs. The original wealth of these tombs must have been staggering. Unfortunately this new method of hiding pharaohs was also to possess only a temporary security: to date only Tutankhamun's tomb has been found almost intact.

Above: Scenes and texts from the *Book of Amduat* ("That which is in the Netherworld") in the burial chamber of the tomb of Thutmose III, in the Valley of the Kings.

The theme of the book concerns the journey of the sun-god through the realms of darkness during the hours of night, culminating in his rebirth with the dawn.

Right: Detail of a wall painting from the tomb of Seti I in the Valley of the Kings. His tomb is, perhaps, the finest in the valley and its quality is the high point of the New Kingdom.

Seti I

1294–1279BC

Seti I — also known as Sethos I and Menmaatra — continued the policies of his recent predecessors, launching new building projects and campaigns to restore the country and its religion to what it had been pre-Armarna.

His reign spanned 13 years and saw another veritable high point of Ancient Egyptian art and culture. Some of the huge projects undertak-

Left and Below: Details of wall reliefs and paintings from Seti I's mortuary temple at Abydos. These superb artworks represent the religious rituals that were carried out in the temple, which was built to reassure the populace that a king hailing from the Delta and named after Set, the God of Destruction, could rightfully rule on the throne of Horus. His unique cult center had shrines to all the major gods and was built out of the finest white limestone, with the reliefs painted in bright colors.

Right: Detail of the astronomical ceiling from the vaulted burial chamber of Seti I's tomb, the longest and finest in the Valley of the Kings.

en included the massive Hypostyle Hall at the Temple of Amun at Karnak, his own temple (with seven sanctuaries), and the Ramesses I temple at Abydos along with the Osireion, and his own tomb and mortuary temple at Thebes. The quality of these projects, right down to the carvings and reliefs, is of a caliber rarely equaled throughout Egypt's long history. His queen, Tuya, was from the same military class and background to himself; she survived him by many years, on into the reign of their son, Ramesses II.

One part of the Seti temple at Abydos has a "politically correct" king list which omits the Amarna kings entirely, with Horembeb following directly after Amenhotep III.

Seti I's tomb in the valley of the Kings is, without doubt, the finest, made to the highest standards, with superior workmanship to most others, and beautifully decorated with the *Book of Gates* and the *Book of Coming Forth by Day*.

His mummy was found in the great Royal Cache at Deir el-Bahari, in good condition, revealing a noble face. Dockets on the mummy record various moves and restorations, following the inevitable desecration of his tomb.

It is interesting to note the assumption of the reviled Set into this king's name. Obviously that god's destructive power and martial spirit were still sometimes acknowledged.

Ramesses II

1279–1213BC

Also known as Usermaatra Setepenra, Ramesses II became Ancient Egypt's best-known and longest-lived pharaoh. He succeeded his father at the age of 25 and reigned over 65 years, outliving even some of his many children. He was a prolific builder, constructing many temples and raising colossal statues and obelisks. He also continued the military tradition of his family, being taken regularly on campaign by his father. In his youth he had two principal wives, Nefertari and Istnofret, by whom he had at least five sons and two daughters. In later life he would boast of over a hundred sons and daughters. Following royal custom Ramesses also took many subsequent wives from his own immediate family, but he also had a cosmopolitan harem including a number of Hittite princesses, as well as Syrian and Babylonian.

Ramessses had inherited a land increasingly drawn into the almost constant jockeying for power that

would become the norm, now that Egypt was no longer cut off and isolated. He also bears the honor of winning, or leading, the Egyptian forces in the first recorded battle in history, at Kadesh against the Hittites.

Seti I had maintained Egyptian influence in the southern end of the Phoenician coastline throughout his reign, but by the fifth year of Ramesses' reign there was a revolt, which Ramesses quickly strove to put down, assembling one of the largest Egyptian armies ever — approximately 20,000 men in four divisions. The army followed the traditional route through the Gaza strip to reach Kadesh in early May. Though the outcome of the battle was not an outright victory, Ramesses saw it as such, because he had a lucky escape and because it did preserve the status quo for another long period.

He recorded the triumph on all his building projects, and it was even used in schools as a boy's exercise. Further campaigns were fought over the years, though these were more of holding operations than attempts at conquest, as both the Egyptians and the Hittites realised that no one could hold it all for long, so a treaty was eventually hammered out and sealed with a Hittite princess. This was repeated seven years later.

Ramesses was certainly the most prolific monument-building pharaoh of them all. Though he appropriated any older statues or buildings he could, hacking off older cartouches and substituting his own, he still built fresh works on a massive scale. Perhaps his greatest achievement is the temple complex at Abu Simbel. He also built a substantial mortuary

Colossal black granite seated statue of Ramesses II wearing the White Crown of Upper Egypt, from the main axis of the temple complex at Luxor. This view looks from the Court of Ramesses II towards the magnificent colonnade of Amenhotep III directly behind the colossus.

temple, the Ramasseum, built on the west bank at Thebes, as well as the largest tomb in the Valley of the Kings, now sadly almost completely derelict. He also added to the temples at Karnak and Luxor, finished his father's mortuary temple at Thebes, and built a magnificent new city, Piramesse, in the delta. This amount of building must have been a considerable drain on resources, and Ramesses must have continually sought the gold and wealth to pay for it.

Finally, after many jubilee festivals, in his 67th regnal year, the great Ramesses went to the west.

His body was found with his father and grandfather in the great Royal Cache at Deir el-Bahari.

Left: Another gargantuan statue of Ramesses II at Luxor is given scale by the tourist. Continuing the pharaonic obsession in size, Ramesses II built on a scale unsurpassed by any following monarch.

Below: Detail of the head of Ramesses II, from another colossal statue at the great temple that he built at Abu Simbel.

MERNEPTAH
1213–1203BC
Merneptah — Also called Baenra Merynetjeru — was middle-aged or more by the time he succeeded his father to the throne. He was the thirteenth son of Ramesses II, and succeeded because many of his brothers had pre-deceased their father. He reigned for 10 years and, given his age, he must have realized that his reign would be relatively short. He began building his mortuary temple at the Theban desert's edge straight away, as well as his tomb in the Valley of the Kings.

Merneptah inherited a peaceful kingdom, though it was not long to remain so: he was soon forced to continue his father's military policy. A revolt in the south of Syria was soon put down, but other more serious threats were beginning to appear. The ancient enemy, the Hittites, with whom Ramesses II had made a kind of working peace, were now under pressure themselves from the north. When their harvest failed they invoked the old treaty and appealed to Merneptah, who sent grain. Next the Libyans on the western frontier began to leave their deserts and increase infiltration of the delta. Merneptah was able to smash these savages quickly and comprehensively, followed by a lightning strike on the Nubians, who had supported the Libyans. The Karnak inscription dated to his reign records these actions, and the fact that Merneptah continued to defend his borders against all-comers.

His tomb lies close to his father's in the Valley of the Kings. Unfinished and robbed, with the usual fragments of *ushabtis* and other funerary equipment, it was empty: his mummy was discovered in the smaller Royal Cache, in the tomb of Amenhotep II.

AMENMESSES
1203–1200BC
There now occurred a hiccup in the succession — perhaps because the co-regent or heir apparent, who would become Seti II, was elsewhere at the time of the old king's death. His place was usurped by Amenmesses (also called Menmira Setepenra), who was, perhaps, a younger prince of the royal line and, therefore, a brother of Seti II. Amenmesses' reign was short — some four years — with the only real evidence of him in the Theban area, where a few fine statues have been found. It is likely that his usurpation was ended suddenly when Seti II succeeded in toppling him. Certainly, his tomb in the Valley of the Kings was officially broken into and defaced, with the cartouches hacked off — another serious attempt to wipe a political enemy from history and deny him eternity as well.

SETI II
1200–1194BC
Seti II — also known as Sethos II and Userkheperura Setepenra — was the rightful successor to Merneptah. Once Set II had outmaneuvered his rival, Amenmesses, he appropriated his monuments and destroyed his tomb. Having attained his inheritance, Seti did not have long to enjoy it and little is known of his short reign, other than that he had three queens were Takhat II, Twosret, and Tiaa. He continued to build at Karnak, as did all this dynasty, but his tomb in the Valley of the Kings was never completed and his mummy was found in the tomb of Amenhotep II.

SIPTAH
1194–1188BC
Seti II's death was followed by yet another succession struggle: it is unclear whether his eldest son had pre-deceased him, or whether he was just outmaneuvered by the Vizier, Bay, who was an adherent of the previous usurper. The result was that Siptah — also known as Saptah and Akhenra Setepenra — the son of Amenmesses, succeeded to the throne. He was only just into his teens, so his stepmother, Twosret (the wife of Seti II), became regent, and the real power behind the throne. When Twosret became more established, she assumed full pharaonic titles and seems to have spirited away Siptah, whose short reign means there are but few monuments attributed to him — at Memphis, Thebes, and in Nubia, including a very distinctive statue of him seated in the lap of Amenmesses.

Siptah's tomb in the Valley of the Kings is incomplete and empty, but his mummy was found in the smaller Royal Cache in the tomb of Amenhotep II. When unwrapped it was found that he had a club foot, the legacy of some childhood illness.

TWOSRET
1188–1186BC
Twosret — also known as Tausret and Sitra Meritamun — swiftly seized her moment and declared herself queen, adopting the full pharaonic titles. She then began a massive extension of her tomb, in keeping with her new rank and pretensions. However, it seems Ma'at was offended as the two brief years of her reign were racked with dissension and civil war. Her tomb in the Valley of the Kings was begun for Siptah while she was regent, but she took it over, just as she, in turn, would be superseded by Setnakte.

So ended the Nineteenth Dynasty, remembered today for its glorious monuments and tombs and the lengthy reign of Ramesses II. But it is obvious that the dynasty founded by Ramesses I struggled to hold its inheritance and civil war was never far from the surface — as was shown again following Twosret's death.

Front view of the Ramesseum, the mortuary temple of Ramesses II which is aligned with the Temple at Luxor but on the opposite bank. It was Shelley's *Tomb of Ozymandias*, inspiring the poem with its colossal sculpture and masonry.

Above: The Ramesseum at Karnak is dedicated to Amun-United-with-Eternity and Ramesses II. The fallen colossus that inspired Selley's poem is just visible on the far right.

Left: The entrance to Ramesses II's temple at Abu Simbel dedicated to himself, the sun-god Ra-Harakte, the stellar god Amun, and Ptah of the Memphite Triad. The four immense statues of the pharaoh dwarf smaller figures around his feet and knees — his wives and daughters — and the image of Ra-Harakte above the doorway. They are each 65½ft (20m) high.

Above Right: Detail from the front of the Temple of Hathor and Nefertari (Ramesses II's queen) at Abu Simbel. This facade has two standing figures of Ramesses II, flanking those of his queen on each side of the entrance.

Below Right: A view of both temples alongside each other. In the 1960s both these rock-hewn temples were threatened by the rising waters of Lake Nasser, a result of the recently completed High Dam at Aswan. In a UNESCO world heritage initiative both temples were dismantled and reassembled on higher ground.

Two more views of Ramesses II's huge temple at Abu Simbel.

The great temple is precisely aligned so that twice yearly — in February and October — the rising sun shines directly through the entrance into the interior, illuminating the seated statues of the gods at the back of the sanctuary. The temple was finished in around the 35th year of the king's reign, and betrays a gradual decline in overall artistic standards, made up for by vigor and — as usual with Ramesses II — its sheer size.

TWENTIETH DYNASTY 1186-1069BC

SETNAKHTE
1186–1184BC

Setnakhte — also known as Userkhaura Setepenra — had a brief reign of only four years. His lineage is not known; perhaps he was like Horembeb, another man for his time — able, almost certainly of a noble/military background, a man who grasped the reins of power at the end of a dynasty that had always struggled to maintain its legitimacy despite its longevity. Such an occasion would also justify the incorporation of Set into the name of a martial pharaoh.

Whatever the reason, following the death of Twosret Egyptian history blurs for a short time until the emergence of Setnakhte. According to the Great Harris Papyrus he put down rebellions, reopened temples, and restored order.

He appropriated his tomb in the Valley of the Kings from Twosret, but his mummy-less coffin was found in the Royal Cache in the tomb of Amenhotep II. Setnakhte's son by his wife Tiye-merenese adopted the name of Ramesses, and would go on to emulate the successes of his namesake.

RAMESSES III
1184–1153BC

Ramesses III — also known as Usermaatra Meryamun — was the last of the truly great pharaohs. He succeeded his father Setnakhte to the throne following a short co-regency, and reigned for just over 30 years. He had at least three main royal wives and some 10 children, many of whom pre-deceased him and were buried in the Valley of the Queens. He inherited a kingdom increasingly involved in a fast-changing world. No longer was Egypt in isolation, only threatened by primitive barbarians who needed to be subdued annually with a show of might. The world was becoming an ever-busier place as a great wave of movement among displaced peoples took place. Mycenaean civilization was overwhelmed, and Egypt's ancient enemy the Hittites were soon to be submerged as well.

Ramesses initially concentrated on consolidating his grip on the throne by continuing his father's work of restoring the country. In about the fifth year of his reign the Libyans, in alliance with at least two other peoples, attacked into the delta from the west, but the Egyptians defeated them easily and enslaved the survivors. The next threat was much more serious: an alliance known as the Sea Peoples, consisting of at least six tribes — Peleset (Philistines), Tjeker, Shekelesh, Sikels, Weshesh, and Denyen — was emigrating eastwards. They overwhelmed the Hittite empire and approached Egypt itself through the overland route, with their fleet keeping pace alongside. The story is recorded in hieroglyphic on the second pylon of Ramesses' mortuary temple at Medinet Habu. They were drawn like others before them to the Nile's lush river banks and delta, with its concomitant quality of life. Ramesses III met their land army at the border and annihilated it. Their fleet remained a threat until it was defeated at the mouth of one of

The mortuary temple of Ramesses III at Medinet Habu. Closely modeled on the Ramesseum, the complex included a small palace in which the pharaoh would stay during festivals. After his death this became the symbolic residence for his spirit. Inside the first court there is a row of colossi of Ramesses III.

the Nile's eastern branches. For a few years following the Sea Peoples' attempted invasion, Ramesses III had a brief respite, but the Libyans were soon trying to invade and settle the western side of the delta. Again they were repulsed with great slaughter.

Ramesses had other problems, too. A fragmentary papyrus records details of a harem conspiracy; a minor queen, Tiy, was the main defendant, she had tried to ensure that her son would succeed to the throne. The conspiracy was discovered and thwarted, though Ramesses actually died before the case was finished.

His tomb in the Valley of the Kings is famous for its paintings. His mummy was found in the Great Cache at Deir el-Bahari.

Ramesses IV

1153–1147BC

Otherwise named as Heqamaatra Setepenamun, Ramesses IV took on an increasingly important role in the closing years of his father's reign. As heir to the throne, the conspiracy against his father would obviously have been aimed at his removal too, so the ferocity of his punishment meted out to the conspirators is perfectly understandable. Having settled this affair he began various building projects, including his never completed mortuary temple and his tomb in the Valley of the Kings. His mother's name is not certain, but he married a Tentopet, who bore him his son and heir. Though a stele at Abydos records his hope of a reign equal in length to his namesake, it was not to be, for he died in his sixth regnal year. His mummy was in the Royal Cache in Amenhotep II's tomb.

Ramesses V

1147–1143BC

Also known as Amenhirkopshef I and Usermaatra Sekheperenra.

Ramesses V was the son of Ramesses III. He, too, had a short reign that lasted about four years. Almost nothing is known about him other than that his wife was called Nubkhesed, he had no surviving children, civil war raged during his reign, and he himself died from smallpox before he could accomplish anything. His mummy was found in the smaller Royal Cache inside Amenhotep II's tomb.

Ramesses VI

1143–1136BC

With the death of Ramsesses V, the throne reverted to his younger brother known as Ramesses VI Amenhirkposhef II, Amenhirkopshef II, and Nebmaatra Meryamun.

He reigned for eight years, during which Egypt was squeezed increasingly from all sides, and forced to give up its near eastern possessions. Ramesses VI's reign would be the last in which the turquoise mines in the Sinai were worked. Certainly the apex of achievement culture shown in the reigns of Ramesses II and III had finished and now was the time of gradual descent.

Ramesses VI took over his predecessor's tomb in the Valley of the King's, but his mummy was found in the Royal Cache in Amenhotep II's tomb. It had been viciously assaulted by robbers, and attempts had been made to repair it, or at least keep as much as possible of it in one place.

Ramesses VII

1136–1129BC

Also known as Usermaatra Meryamun Setepenra, Ramesses VII was the son of Ramesses VI. He succeeded his father in 1183BC and reigned for about seven years, about which little is known. Nothing is known of Ramesses VII's wives or children, but it seems that tragedy struck when the pharaoh's son predeceased him. Inexorably Egypt teetered on the brink of catastrophe — a catastrophe of its own making. Despite the success of individual reigns, a firm monarchy had not been established. There was rampant inflation and the tired old systems began to fail.

Ramesses VII's tomb was robbed in ancient times and no remains of his mummy have ever been discovered.

Ramesses VIII

1129–1126BC

Also known as Sethirkopshef and

Steps leading down to the entrance of the tomb of Ramesses VI. This tomb had originally been prepared for his predecessor, but was usurped by Ramesses VI. His mummy was discovered in the smaller Royal Cache within the tomb of Amenhotep II.

Usermaatra Akhenamun, Ramesses VIII was yet another son of Ramesses III. Unlike his father, Ramesses VIII only ruled for a single year and the whereabouts of his tomb and body are unknown.

It is difficult without clear evidence to understand the minutiae of royal succession at this time. There's no doubt that Ramesses VIII was an aging prince of the royal bloodline: however, his successor's antecedents are unknown.

RAMESSES IX
1126–1108BC
Ramesses IX — also named Neferkhara Setepenra — ruled for some 18 years and so brought a measure of continuity after the succession problems following the death of Ramesses III. Despite this, little remains of his reign except at Heliopolis in the Delta. Thebes and the powerful priests of the great temple were left increasingly to their own devices, a source of growing future problems: one of which was the plundering of the Valley of the Kings.

Ramesses IX's syringe tunnel-tomb is opposite that of Ramesses II. His mummy was found in the great Royal Cache at Deir el-Bahari.

RAMESSES X
1108–1099BC
Very little is known about this pharaoh, who is also known as Khepermaatra Setepenra, other than that his reign lasted some seven or eight years. His tomb in the Valley of the Kings was empty and his mummy has never been found.

RAMESSES XI
1099–1069BC
Also known as Menmaatra Setepenptah, the final Ramesses and final pharaoh of this dynasty, Ramesses XI reigned for almost 30 years, and left behind more traces of his reign than his immediate predecessors. Papyri record the increasing volatility of the time and the breakdown of law and order, as the internal strife that dogged the nineteenth and twentieth dynasties made itself apparent again.

Ramesses ruled from his capital Piramesse in the delta, where he could oversee and try to deal with the emerging and hungry Mediterranean world. The country was still divided into three provinces: the pharaoh in the north, a viceroy of Kush — Panhesy — in the deep south, and the high priest of Amun in the great temple at Thebes. After almost 2,000 years the temple was bloated with the wealth showered upon Amun by grateful pharaohs in recompense for victory. The high priests had gradually become so powerful that they challenged the very right of the pharaohs to rule them. And so once more Egypt's latent duality became an issue once more as civil war broke out between north and south.

In Ramesses' twefth regnal year the priest of Amun disappeared and the viceroy of Kush, Panhesy, replaced him. He was replaced by Herihor, who, despite his military origins, eventually became high priest. By Ramesses' nineteenth regnal year, Panhesy had disappeared, his titles claimed by Herihor, whose ambition was revealed in his construction of a temple to Khons, the Theban moon-god. The reliefs on this temple show Herihor equal in size to the king and his name within a royal cartouche — high priest had become priest-king and it appears that Ramesses XI couldn't do anything about it. Pharaonic control of the Two Lands had broken down and another period of chaos ensued.

To add insult to injury, when Ramesses XI's tomb in the Valley of the Kings was excavated, it was found never to have been used for his burial, but as a workshop through which royal mummies passed, being stripped of their gold and jewels before being cached in new hiding places. Ramesses XI's body has never been found.

THE THIRD INTERMEDIATE PERIOD 1069-525BC

HIGH-PRIEST KINGS AT THEBES

HERIHOR
1080–1074BC
The priesthood of the temple at Thebes was now wealthy and strong enough to make a bid for power in its own right. As has been seen, this power reached its height in the reign of Ramesses XI, when Herihor gave up all pretence of submission to the pharaoh, and ruled southern Egypt as his own fief. He was also called Hemnetjertepyenamun and Siamun and he died some six years before Rameses XI. His main building work was the temple of the moon-god Khons on the south side of the temple-complex at Karnak. The mummy of his wife, Nodjmet, was found in the Royal Cache at Deir el-Bahari, but no tomb or mummy attributed to him has been found.

PIANKH
1074–1070BC
Piankh had a short reign, with no regnal years of his own, using those of Ramesses XI, with whom he co-

existed. They both died at around the same time. Piankh did not use the royal cartouche around his name either.

PINEDJEM I

1070–1032BC

Piankh was succeeded by his son, Pinedjem, who was also known as Khakheperra Setepenamun. As with Piankh, Pinedjem I had no regnal years of his own, but followed instead those of the pharaoh in the delta (Smendes I). He appears on a pylon in the temple complex at Karnak, and put his name on a colossal statue of Rameses II.

In order to unite the two ruling families of the north and south, Pinedjem married Henuttawy, a daughter of Ramesses XI: some of their offspring would become pharaohs, others high priests.

Pinedjem's mummy was found in the Royal Cache at Deir el-Bahari.

MASAHERTA

1054–1046BC

Only the body discovered in the great Royal Cache at Deir el-Bahari proves this priest-king's existence; nothing else is known about him.

MENKHEPERRA

1045–992BC

Also called Hemnetjertepyenamun, almost no trace of this priest-king exists , other than his listing at Thebes and his name, along with that of Pinedjem I, printed on bricks at the ruined fortress and the temple of Amun at el-Hiba.

SMENDES II

992–990BC

Son of Masaherta, Smendes's mummy was found with his father's in the great Royal Cache; nothing else is known about this priest-king. The survival of these mummies is due to precautions taken by the Theban priesthood, who rescued and relocated as many remains of pharaohs and priest-kings they could once the integrity of the Theban necropolis had been compromised.

PINEDJEM II

990–969BC

The son of Menkheperra, Pinedjem II was also known as Khakheperra Stepenamun.. His mummy was found in the Royal Cache at Deir el-Bahari, together with that of his wife, Neskhons.

PSUSENNES III

969–945BC

Probably the son of Pinedjem II, although this is by no means certain, his mummy was found in the Deir el-Bahari Royal Cache.

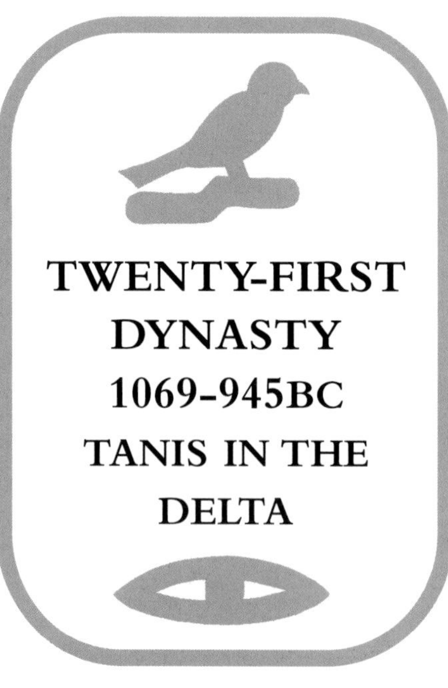

SMENDES I

1069–1043BC

Although no discernible relation to Ramesses XI, Smendes — also known as Hedjkheperra Setepenra — proclaimed himself king following Ramesses XI's death and marryied one of the pharaoh's numerous daughters to bolster his claim. During his reign the delta capital was moved from Piramesse to Tanis. Smendes also carried out restoration work at the great temple at Karnak.

AMENEMNISU

1043–1039BC

Also known as Neferkara, Amenemisu was a son of the first high priest-king Herihor and his wife Nodjmet, a dynastic link between the Two Lands.

PSUSENNES I

1039–991BC

Also named Akheperra Setepenamun, Psusennes I's primary claim to fame is that his tomb at Tanis is the only tomb of a pharaoh ever found intact and unscathed, though his mummy had decayed due to either bad preservative techniques or Delta dampness. Mutnodjmet, his wife, was buried with him. Psusennes kept the links with Thebes by marrying his daughter Isiemkheb to the High Priest Menkheperra.

AMENEMOPE

993–984BC

Also called Usermaatra Meryamun Setepenamun, Amenemope was the son of Psusennes I, and was buried in the same site at Tanis.

OSORKON (THE ELDER)

984–978BC

Also called Aakheperra Setepenra. Almost no evidence exists for this king other than his names.

SIAMUN

978–959BC

Also Netjerkheperra Setepenamun. Siamun reigned for almost 20 years. He built at Piramesse and at Tanis in the delta, and also at Thebes.

PSUSENNES II

959–945BC

Also known as Titkheperura; little is known about him or his reign.

View through the first pylon at the Temple of Luxor, with a seated Ramesses II and the sole remaining obelisk — the second now graces the Place de la Concorde in Paris.

Above: Looking across a court to the Hypostyle Hall at the Temple of Luxor, a veritable forest of columns.

Left: A row of human-headed sphinxes leading to the temple entrance at Luxor. They bear the cartouche of Thirtieth Dynasty pharaoh Nakhtnebef, whom the Greeks knew as Nectanebo I.

These processional ways were used on festival days to lead cult statues in and out of the sacred grounds.

Right: A closer view of Luxor's Hypostyle Hall from amongst its huge columns. The transition through pylon and court to the hypostyle hall of a temple had a specific religious significance — it was interpreted as mirroring the process of creation. The hall itself symbolized the reed swamp that grew on the fringes of the primeval mound.

Above: The floodlit main processional route lined with criosphinxes leading to the massive first pylon at the great temple complex of Amun-Ra at Karnak.

This pylon is the largest ever built in Ancient Egypt. It dates from the Thirtieth Dynasty, and is almost 131ft (40m) high. Perhaps in part because of its massive scale, it was never completely finished, with much of the walls left undressed and even partial remains of the mudbrick ramp used in its construction still evident.

Left: Another colossal seated statue of Ramesses II at Karnak. This temple complex represents 1,500 years of accretion, becoming one of the largest and most impressive religious monuments of all time, anywhere in the world.

Right: A view of the court of Ramesses II with the chapel of Thutmose III at the Temple of Luxor.

Above: Looking across to the columns and architraves of the processional colonnade built by Amenhotep III at the temple to the Theban Triad — Amun, Mut, and Khons — at Luxor. Built mainly from the time of the New Kingdom onwards, this temple has a simpler and more cohesive structure than its huge haphazard neighbor at Karnak.

Right: Looking up at the massive architrave lintels on top of papyrus bud capitals in the court of Amenhotep III at the temple at Luxor.

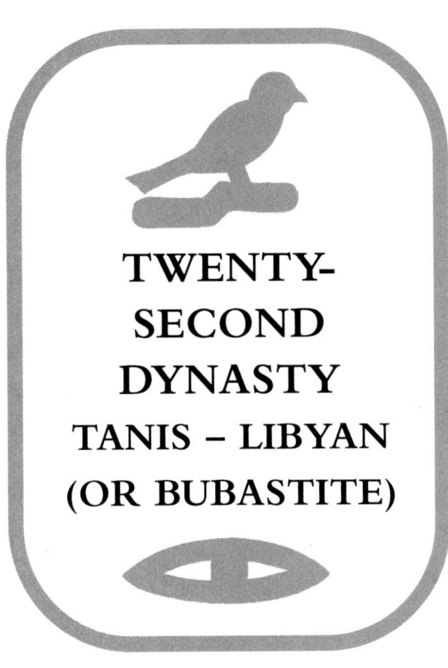

SHESHONQ I
945–924BC
Also called Hedjkheperra Setepenra, Sheshonq I came from a Libyan military background — for many years Libyans and other foreigners had been settling in the delta and adopting the native Egyptian ways. Seshonq I allied himself to the previous dynasty and legitimized his claim by marrying Maatkara, the daughter of Psusennes II.

His strength and military expertise once more united the country, and he placed his sons in key positions of power and authority. One son, Iuput, was the governor of Upper Egypt and high priest of Amun, with another brother, Djedptahaufankh, backing him up as third priest of Amun. Another son, Nimlot, was the military commander of Herakleopolis.

In 930BC, with Judah and Israel in dispute following the death of Solomon, Sheshonq saw his chance and invaded. He defeated both nations in a magnificent campaign celebrated on the walls of the great temple of Amun at Thebes. He patronized various temples in Tanis and Bubastis in the Delta and commissioned more work at Karnak.

Sheshonq died soon after his Palestinian campaigns, and was buried in the royal burial ground at Tanis.

OSORKON I (SHESHONQ II)
c.890BC
Also called Heqakheperra Setepenra, Osorkon I was the son of Sheshonq II. He continued his father's policy of putting sons into the priesthood to consolidate his position, replacing Iuput with one of his own sons also named Sheshonq. He took this son as his co-regent but Sheshonq (callthe Second) did not succeed to the throne, dying before him. Both were buried in the royal tombs at Tanis.

TAKELOT I
889–874BC
Also called Usermaatra Stepenra, Takelot I was another son of Osorkon I by a lesser wife. His reign has left little to posterity, other than that the Two Lands began to fragment again.

OSORKON II
874–850BC
Osorkon II, also known as Hedjkheperra Setepenra, came to the throne at about the same time as his cousin Harsiese inherited the high priesthood from his father Seshonq II. Harsiese soon declared himself pharaoh of the south and Osorkon had to wait until Harsiese's death some years later before he could place his own son, Nimlot, as high priest and another son, Sheshonq, as high priest of Ptah at Memphis.

Osorkon II undertook various building and restoration work at Tanis, Thebes, Memphis, Leontopolis, and Bubastis, with special emphasis on the latter (his home city) at the temple of the cat-goddess Bastet. Osorkon II also allied himself with various erstwhile enemies to defeat the Assyrians.

TAKELOT II
850–825BC
Takelot — also named Hedjkheperra Setepenra — succeeded his father to the throne. The north and south were bonded in alliance through the marriage of Takelot to Karomama, a daughter of his half-brother Nimlot, the High Priest of Amun at Karnak. But unity between Thebes and the delta was short-lived. When Nimlot died, the Thebans rebelled against Takelot's choice of his son, Osorkon, for the office of high priest, preferring their own Harsiese. The rebels were destroyed by Takelot; a brief period of peace followed before rebellion broke out again.

On his death Takelot was buried at Tanis; his mummy was found in the tomb of Osorkon II.

SHESHONQ III
825–773BC
Takelot's eldest son and heir-apparent, Osorkon, never reigned, pipped at the post by his younger brother, who seized the throne becoming Sheshonq III (also known as Usermaatra Setepenra).

His reign lasted over 50 years and saw a breakdown of Egypt into composite city-states. The Thebans chose Harsiese as high priest, though he later appointed his older brother.

In about Sheshonq III's eighth regnal year a prince of Leontopolis named Pedibastet proclaimed himself king of a new (Twenty-Third) dynasty. He was joined by some of the rebel Theban priests of Amun. Pedibastet, Sheshonq IV, and Osorkon III all ruled at Leontopolis during Sheshonq III's reign.

PAMI
773–767BC
Almost nothing known about this king, other than his alternative name of Usermaatra Setepenamun.

SHESHONQ V
767–730BC
The son of Pami, he was also known as Aakheperra.

OSORKON IV
870–860BC
Also named Aakheperra Setepanamun. He was the son of Sheshonq V.

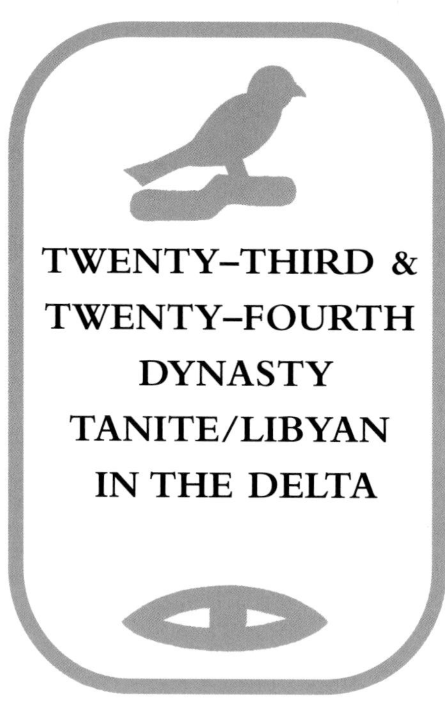

The complexity of this period in Egyptian history is made worse by the fragmentation of the kingdom of the Two Lands into what were effectively city states. Intermarriage, the similarity of names, the mixture of high priests and pharaohs, all these conspire against a definitive history. That being said, the trends are more straightforward: the Libyan Twenty-Second Dynasty ruled an Eygpt that had contracted in size from the earliest days, and whose neighbors, particularly Nubia, were growing in power . This position would worsen during the rule of the Twenty-Third and Twenty-Fourth Dynasties until outright war with Nubia would take place. Defeat of the Egyptian army would lead, ultimately, to a Nubian dynasty — the Twenty-Fifth.

Pedibastet
818–793BC

Sheshonq IV
793–787BC

Osorkon III
787–759BC

Rudamon
757–754BC

Iuput
754–715BC
Also called Usermaatra

AT HERAKLEOPOLIS

Peftjauabastet
Also called Neferkara.

AT HERMOPOLIS

Nimlot

AT SAIS IN THE DELTA

Tefnakht
727–720BC
The growing Nubian–Kushite power in the south at last impinged on the consciousness of a leader in the delta and was seen as a serious threat. Tefnakht — also called Shepsesra — was one of the first to attempt a coalition of delta kings. He united with Osorkon IV in Tanis, Nimlot of Hermopolis, Iuput of Leontopolis and Peftjauabastet in Herakleopolis.

Initially they contained the Kushite king, Piankhi, but later the two sides fought at Herakleopolis where the northern coalition was defeated and forced to surrender. Pianki allowed them to continue in their roles as city-state kings, but the writing was on the wall.

Bakenrenef
720–715BC
Bakenrenef — also called Wahkara — succeeded Tefnakht to the kingship of Sais under the overlordship of Piankhi. He is the only universally recognized pharaoh of the Twenty-Fourth Dynasty; some Egyptologists suggest that Tefnakht was the first.

Right: The remains of the ruined kiosk of Taharqa, a Nubian pharaoh of the Twenty-Fifth Dynasty. It originally stood some 86¾ft (26.5m) high and consisted of 10 massive open papyrus columns with entrances to the east and west. Now all that remains is this one partly reconstructed pillar and a huge alabaster altar.

Nubia, for so long a despised colony, had evolved considerably since the time of the New Kingdom. But Egyptian culture had been the seed and inspiration. With the cult of Amun firmly established, the priesthood, like its Theban counterpart, grew in power until they married into and took over the Nubian kingship based at Napata. The kingdom of Napata flourished and as Egyptian power waned, so the Kushites looked to expand north, perhaps even to reassert the ascendancy of Amun over the various gods of the delta cities.

Piankhi
747–716BC
Also called Menkheperra.
Piankhi was the High Priest of Amun at the cult's center at Gebel Barkal. He married the daughter of the seventh king of Napata, Alara, and succeeded to the throne on that king's death. His influence steadily increased to the north as the delta kings squabbled and maneuvered, and he was well received in Thebes.

In about his twentieth regnal year, Piankhi moved against the coalition of northern kings, defeating them at Herakleopolis. He established his influence at Thebes by getting his sister adopted as the Divine Adoratrice of Amun, and instigating building and restoration work at the great temple, but he preferred to rule from Napata. On his death, he was buried in a Kushite pyramid at Gebel Barkal.

SHABAKA

716–702BC

The brother of Piankhi, whom he succeeded to the throne, Shabaka (also called Neferkara) continued to exert Kushite influence in Egypt proper. He, too, undertook extensive building and restoration of various cults, mainly Amun at Thebes but also at Dendera, Esna, Edfu, Abydos, and Memphis. During his reign the threat from the Assyrian Empire continued to grow, but Shabaka managed to contain it. He was buried at the Kushite royal burial ground near the cult center of Gebel Barkal.

SHEBITKU

702–690BC

Also called Djedkara, Shebitku was the nephew of Shabaka and a son of Piankh. Shebitku had a more complicated part to play against the outside threat, making an alliance with Palestinians and Phoenicians against Assyrian overlordship, but they were soon defeated by the Assyrian king Sennacherib.

TAHARQA

690–664BC

Taharqa, who was also called Nefertemkhura, succeeded his brother Shebitku to the throne. The Assyrian threat faded slightly with Sennacherib's death in 681BC, but it was soon to resume, and would continue throughout Taharqa's reign. In 673BC the Assyrians were thrown back at the border, but in 671BC they successfully invaded, taking Memphis.

Taharqa was forced to flee to Thebes, from where he led a brief resurgence against the Assyrians before he was beaten back again — eventually retreating all the way to Napata.

Taharqa built throughout Egypt and Nubia, restoring the temples belonging to many cults, especially at Thebes, the spiritual center of the Napatan priest-kings. His overseer there, Mentuemhet, was made mayor of the city and with various brothers he held the Theban nobility in check.

TANUTAMUN

664–656BC

Shabaka acknowledged his cousin Tanutamun as heir and co-regent a year before his death. Tanutamun (also called Bakare) had high hopes of liberating the whole country and he was initially successful as he pushed north; Thebes and Memphis were again retaken, but the triumph was short-lived. The Assyrian counterattack was devastating and he was pushed all the way back, finally having to flee into the deep south, returning to Napata, where the Assyrians would not pursue him. They did, however, sack Thebes and the great temple, an action that reverberated throughout the ancient world.

With Tanutamun's death in 656BC Kushite power and influence within Egypt came to a close and the Two Lands were dominated by the Assyrians.

Again two dynasties overlapped in different parts of the country, the Twenty-Fifth in the south, and the Twenty-Sixth in the north. As the Assyrians pushed back the Kushites and sacked Thebes in 665BC, they acknowledged Nekau as king of Sais and his son Psamtik as king of Athribis, also in the Delta.

Psamtik I

664–610BC

With the death of his father and the expulsion of the Kushites, Psamtik — also called Wahibra — was made king of the whole country by the Assyrians. He was given the brief of pacifying it all and coming to terms with Thebes. This rapprochement was managed with less effort than anticipated, for the old noble Mentuemhet was still powerful in the Theban nome. Mentuemhet cemented the alliance by enabling Psamtik's daughter Nitocret to become Divine Adoratrice of Amun.

This accommodation with Thebes allowed Psamtik I to turn his attentions to his opponents and rivals in the delta. Gathering together a large army, many of them Greek mercenaries, he soon had the delta under control. His reign of over half a century brought a modicum of peace and stability to an Egypt exhausted and depleted by war. There followed a renaissance of the old styles and ways that to this day can be confusing when attempting to date artifacts.

Finally, as Assyrian power waned, Psamtik was able to cast off the invaders' yoke and once more Egypt was independent. But the world was in ferment and other peoples were eyeing Egyptian land and riches. The Babylonians began to destroy Assyria, and Psamtik even attempted to help his erstwhile enemy, realizing the danger of a power vacuum in the near east, but the Assyrian capital fell in 612BC and the future for Egypt looked ominous.

Nekau

610–595BC

Nekau — also called Wahemibra — inherited the throne from his father, continuing his policies and retaking part of Palestine in an effort to establish a buffer zone against the Babylonians as well as a sphere of influence. Again using Greek mercenaries, he formed a navy and made a navigable link between the Nile Delta and the Red Sea.

Psamtik II

595–589BC

Psamtik II was the son of Nekau and also called Neferibra. He reigned for a short period and there are very few archaeological records with which to substantiate his reign. He does seem to have led some kind of punitive expedition beyond Aswan, but there are only little bits of graffiti left by mercenaries on various monuments to confirm this. He also continued Egyptian involvement in Palestine, supporting an unsuccessful Judaean rebellion against the Babylonians.

Ankhesneferibra, the daughter of Psamtik, was adopted by the Divine Adoratrice Nitocret, taking on the position in her turn: she would hold it for some 60 years, consolidating the dynasty's influence in Thebes until the Persian conquest.

Wahibra

589–570BC

Also called Haaibra, Wahibra inherited the throne from his father, Psamtik II. His reign was plagued with military problems beginning with a rebellion of the garrison at the First Cataract, Aswan, in the south. When Wahibra sent an army to help the Libyans against the invaders it was defeated, and on its return he was challenged by Ahmose, who defeated him. Wahibra died on the battlefield and Ahmose claimed the throne, but he buried his predecessor with all the correct procedures.

Ahmose II

570–526BC

Ahmose II, also called Amasis II and Khnemibra —continued the policies of his predecessors, giving the Greeks a city in the delta and using their talents in warfare to increase his own military power. The influence of Greece was strong around the Mediterranean by this time — although not as strong as it would get — and dealing so closely with them was a double-edged sword: close ties would lead to the Hellenization of the country. Ahmose II had little choice, Egypt was no longer initiating events but reacting to them, and the Persians posed a more immediate threat.

Psamtik III

526–525BC

It is not known whether Psamtik II (also called Ankhara) was a son or relative of Ahmose II, or whether he was related to the earlier family of the Twenty-Sixth Dynasty. He barely had succeeded to the throne before the Persians arrived at Egypt's eastern border, having used Bedouin nomad guides to negotiate the dangerous desert routes across Sinai. Facing such an experienced enemy, Psamtik III was quickly defeated. He fled to Memphis where he was captured and sent in chains to the Persian capital at Susa.

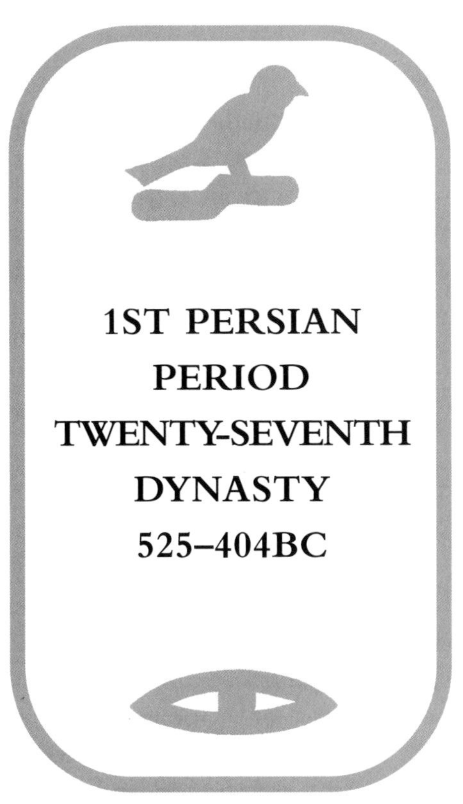

1ST PERSIAN PERIOD TWENTY-SEVENTH DYNASTY 525–404BC

Cambyses II

525–522BC

With the capture of Psamtik, Persian emperor Cambyses found himself master of Egypt and a culture the Persians had little experience or interest in; it was simply a country fabled for its wealth, fertility, and antiquity that the Persians could milk.

Our sources for the Persian occupation of Egypt come from Greece and are therefore rather biased. They accuse the Persians of wilful neglect and cruelty and it is difficult to see beyond this to the truth. It is true that the Persians would not have been as fascinated with this ancient culture as the Greeks undoubtedly were, but the Persian Empire was pragmatic: conquered land had to produce wealth, and a warrior-king such as Cambyses would have conquered the enemy as expediently as possible, and then got things back to normal and profitability as soon as he could.

As far as his position as pharaoh is concerned, his name does appear in cartouche form, with a throne name (he was called Mesutira in Egypt) but little other primary evidence exists to show the results of his reign.

The Persians were much resented by the indigenous Egyptians, although as Persian monarchs went, Darius was exceptionally tolerant of his different subjects' religions. Nevertheless, as soon as the opportunity arose, the Egyptians rebelled against their Persian overlords.

Darius I

521–486BC

When Darius (known as Egypt as Setutra) took over from Cambyses, the Persian Empire was well established and so he could afford to take more of an interest and involvement in the workings of his dominions. As an example of this, he tried and executed Aryandes, the Satrap of Egypt, for corruption and malpractice.

It is also recorded that Darius initiated numerous assorted building and restoration projects throughout the country — from a new temples to the completion of Necho II's canal to the Red Sea in the eastern Delta. His name on reliefs is written in cartouche with an accompanying throne name. When the Greeks under Leonidas defeated the Persians at the Battle of Marathon in 490BC, the irresistible opportunity arose to rebel, which the Egyptians promptly did.

XERXES

485–465BC

Persian attention was briefly caught elsewhere, but when Xerxes came to the throne he soon set about reconquering Egypt ruthlessly. But he, too, would have the unruly, free-spirited Greeks to contend with, and he had to appoint his son Achaemenes as satrap. His cruelty and arrogance did not endear him to the native population and as soon as the news came through that Xerxes had been assassinated, the Egyptians rebelled again.

ARTAXERXES I

464–424BC

When Artaxerxes I came to the Persian throne, a number of Egyptian princes took the opportunity to form an alliance to confront him and rid Egypt of the Persians. They were led by Amyrtaeus of Sais and Inaros of Heliopolis, the son of Psamtik III. They hoped to be able to defeat the Persians with the aid of Greek mercenaries, but although the allies were initially successful, they were eventually defeated and had to revert to guerilla warfare.

During this campaign Inaros was caught and executed and Amyrtaeus driven underground.

DARIUS II

423–405BC

With Darius on the Persian throne, rebellion, always simmering just under the surface in Egypt, erupted again. The main focus of unrest was the delta, where Greek influence and manpower was strongest and where the Tanite and Saite princes still remembered their glorious past.

ARTAXERXES II

405–359BC

With the death of Darius, Artaxerxes II came to the throne; simultaneously in Egypt Amyrtaeus of Sais declared himself king. For the remaining period of this first Persian occupation of Ancient Egypt the pendulum swung back and forth between the country's independence

and occupation. There was always someone prepared to cast off the hated Persian yoke and seek autonomy, but Persian power held sway for nearly a century.

Amyrtaeus
404–399BC
Amyrtaeus came from a line of Saite nobility that had been trying to free themselves from Persian domination for many years. His relatives had died trying to free the country from foreign rule and he himself had been fighting a constant guerrilla war against the forces of occupation. Now, on the death of Darius II, he declared himself king and was accepted by his people.

His authority stretched all the way to Aswan in the south but was held only briefly. He is the only king of the Twenty-Eighth Dynasty, there is no record of his cartouche or other royal names; on top of this, the circumstances of his death are a mystery.

Xerxes was an accomplished soldier and general, who quickly brought Egypt to heel, though there was never any real cultural communication between the two races.

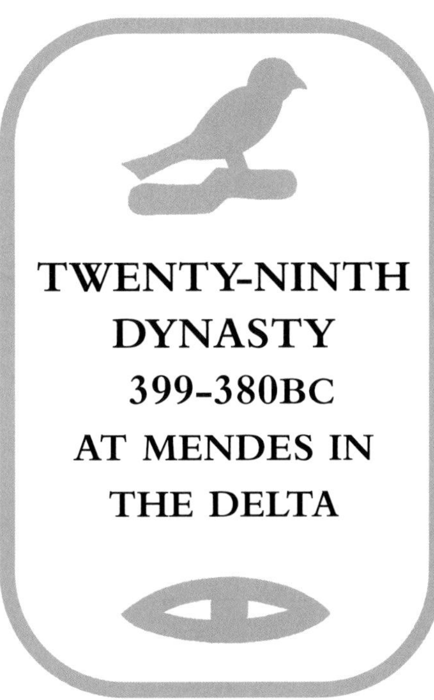

Nefaarud I
399–393BC
Also known as Baenre Merynetjeru, Nefaarud I was no relation to the Saite Amyrtaeus. He was the founder of a new dynasty that based itself in Mendes, a city located in the central delta. Much building and restoration work was carried out during his reign both in the delta and throughout the country, and he is known to have maintained the Apis bull cult at Memphis. His tomb has never been found, but is presumed to be in Mendes, where some of his Ushabti figures were found.

Hakor
393–380BC
Following the death of Nefaarud there was a struggle for the throne between his son and a pretender. In the end neither won, for the throne was taken by Hakor — also known as Maatibra — who tried to legitimize his own rule by associating his name with that of his predecessor.

His reign saw more building and renovation work throughout the country. Hakor also kept a close watch on the near east, fomenting revolution against Persia and, with Greek assistance, building up his navy as much as possible. When the mainland Greeks were bought off by Artaxerxes II, Egypt was left to fight on her own against Persia with just her own army and some mercenaries. Despite this Hakor managed to beat back a number of Persian attacks before he died; his tomb and mummy remain unfound.

Nakhtnebef
380–362BC
Also known as Kheperkara, and in Greek form as Nectanebo I.

When Hakor died in 380BC his son was beaten to the throne by the next man of the moment, Nakhtnebef, a prince of Sebennytos who founded the Thirtieth Dynasty. He was immediately in trouble when Persian and Greek forces invaded the country. Unusually, they entered the delta from a westerly direction, bypassing the heavy eastern defences and defeated Nakhtnebef in battle. He fled south to Memphis where he had time to regroup the Egyptian forces while the ill-suited allies warily squabbled and followed him only slowly. It was in the time of the annual inundation, and such conditions favored those who understood them. Nakhtnebef managed to launch a successful counter-attack, chasing the invaders right out of the country. He then set about restoring the country, instigating many building and restoration projects, including the first temple on the island of Philae.

His chief wife and the mother of his successor was Udjashu. It is not known where his tomb lies

DJEDHOR

362–360BC

Nakhtnebef was succeeded by his son, Djedhor, who was also known as Irmaatenra and, in Greek form, as Teos. He continued his father's military policy against Persia. He also continued to recruit heavily Greek mercenaries for use in his operations against the Persians, and consequently had to raise taxes to pay for them to such a level that he became deeply unpopular. Even though Egypt was not a monetary state, the king had to have gold with which to press up a coinage to pay the mercenaries. In the end, while he was in Palestine, his son, Tjahepimu, declared his own son (and Djedhor's grandson) king. Djedhor then fled to the Persian court at Susa.

NAKHTHOREB

360–343BC

Known in Greek form as Nectanebo II and Egyptian as Snedjemibra Setepeninhur, Nakhthoreb was thrust onto the throne by his father — thereby toppling his grandfather Djedhor. Nakhthoreb had a brief respite from outside interference as the Persian succession went into a murderous internecine mode, but when Artaxerxes III won his supremacy he began to reimpose Persian rule over his ailing empire until, finally, he launched an expedition to reclaim Egypt. It ended in failure, encouraging others to rebel and winning Nakhthoreb more breathing space. There was another traditionalist revival, with temples restored and correct worship of the old gods revived.

However, it was not to last. Both sides were now using the belligerent Greeks as mercenaries when they met on the Egyptian border in 343BC. Those fighting for the Persians outmaneuvered their compatriots fighting with the Egyptians and the great fortress of Pelusium fell. Others in the cities of the Delta followed in turn, with Memphis soon afterwards. Nakhthoreb's reign had come to an end and he fled south into Nubia.

Although it may not have seemed so at the time, this event was a momentous one. Despite conquest and subjugation by various enemies over the recent centuries, Egypt had always been Egyptian and had always won back her freedom. It would not happen again. Nakhthoreb's defeat signalled the end of the reign of the last truly Egyptian pharaoh. The office, and the rituals around it, would continue for some centuries based around the conquerors, and, indeed, there would be much building and wealth — but for there would be no return to old ways: Greece and, ultimately, Rome were to be the powers that mattered now,

Close up of the processional avenue of criosphinxes, which formed the main entrance leading to the massive First Pylon and on into the great temple complex at Karnak.

Sphinxes could have many different types of head including that of a human, ram (called criosphinxes), or or hawk (hierakosphinxes). Sometimes the more usual lion's body and tail was replaced by that of a crocodile.

The Egyptian sphinxes were benevolent, associated with royalty and the sun-god, and were used occasionally as guardians of necropoli. They did not possess the malignancy of their Greek counterparts.

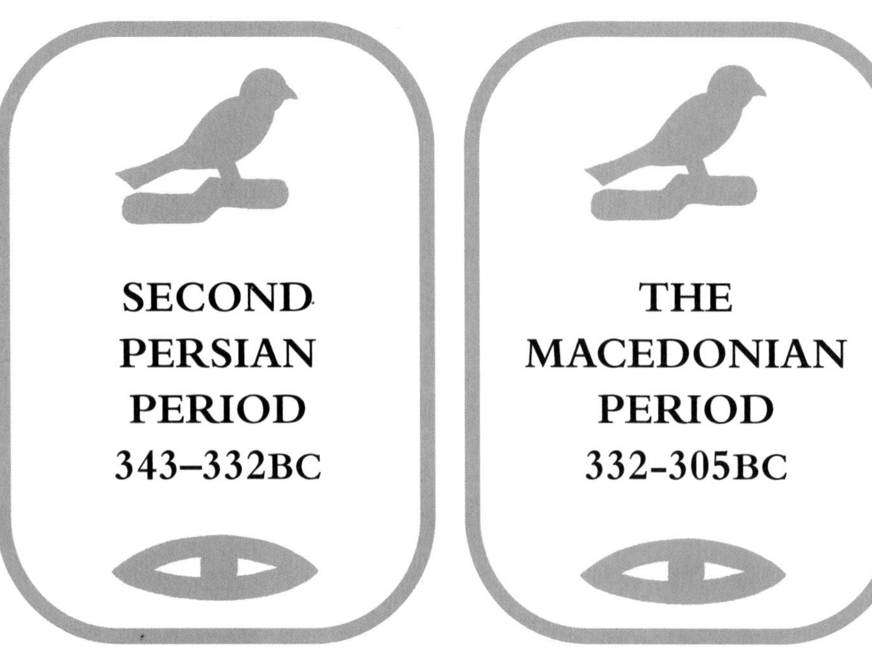

This Second Persian Period would last for only a decade and see three rulers.

Artaxerxes III
343–338BC
With the defeat of Nakhthoreb, Egypt once again became a part of the Persian Empire. It is reported, again mainly from Greek sources, that they wreaked a terrible vengeance on the populace, and poured scorn on the religion and its temples and rituals. Those who had taken part in the rebellion were punished and opposition crushed, funds extorted, and property confiscated. Artaxerxes is known to have had silver coinage struck at Memphis.

Arses
338–336BC
Arses probably never even got time to visit Egypt. He was poisoned within two years of coming to the throne.

Darius III
336–332BC
The Satrap of Egypt under Darius was Mazaeus. He too had a coinage struck, and it was he who decided to cede the satrapy to the next conqueror, Alexander III of Macedon, otherwise known as Alexander the Great.

Across the Mediterranean, classical Greece was being eclipsed as the age of Hellenism arrived, similar in effect in many ways to the rise of the Kushite Napatan Dynasty — a satellite country bordering the principal, steeped in its culture over the years, finally superseded the mother country. So, too, with Macedon. Alexander the Great's father, Philip, had grown up as a political hostage in Thebes and was consequently Hellenic in outlook. He fought as a Greek and ruled as a Greek. So, too, Alexander, who was educated by Aristotle and other great classical poets, philosophers, and scientists. He had been inculcated in their precepts of what should comprise a philosopher king. On top of this he had his father's astute military and political skills allied to the wild energy and toughness of a mountain people. Having managed to tame Greece without destroying its essential spirit, he harnessed it instead to what amounted to a jihad across the Ancient World.

When Alexander led the Greek coalition across into Asia Minor there began a steamroller of Greek culture that, combined later with Semitic monotheism and Roman law, would be a linchpin of the development of the modern world.

Alexander III (the Great)
332–323BC
Also known as Meryamun Setepenra. Having defeated the army of the Persian King Darius completely at Issus in 333BC, Alexander entered Egypt in 332BC. Following a prophecy confirming his divine status, and his own certainty in its truth, he traveled to the ancient oracle of Amun (whom the Greeks identified as Zeus) at Siwa, where he was acknowledged as the rightful divine ruler of Egypt. He was greeted as a savior by the native population and, as he traveled down the Nile, each city swore allegiance to him. When he reached the Delta, he founded

Above: Alexander the Great, acclaimed by the Ancient Egyptians as a rightful ruler and son of a God. The Egyptians welcomed him with open arms as a savior from the hated Persians.

Right: Alexander greeting the royal family of Darius after his defeat of the Persian king at the battle of Issus.

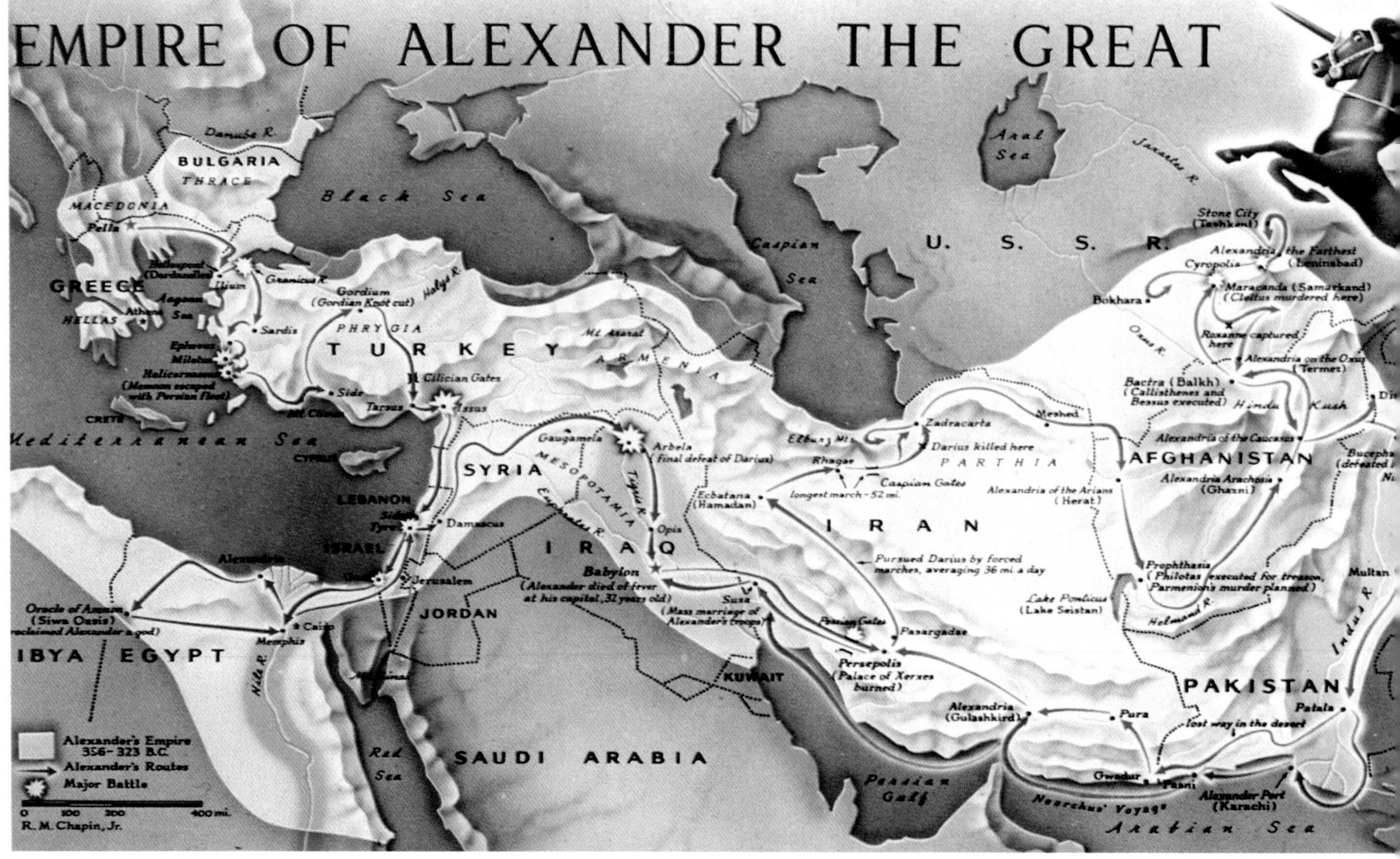

A map of the extent of Alexander the Great's Empire — almost the whole of the known world at that time. As the achievement of one man before the age of 30, it was astonishing and has no rival before or since in any recorded history.

Alexander made great efforts to incorporate all these different races and countries into a cohesive whole and, had he lived, he undoubtedly would have achieved even more.

Alexandria, the first and the greatest of many cities bearing his name — in fact it would become one of the ancient world's most glittering and creative cities, a meeting point of cultures and birthplace of ideas.

It was not long, though, before Alexander had to move on to continue his dream of uniting all peoples into one colossal empire. Yet still he had a lasting effect on Egypt, not the least of which was the inauguration of a great period of rebuilding across the country — temples that had been destroyed by the Persians were rebuilt and the Great Temple at Thebes underwent significant renovation. To underline Alexander's involvement there were reliefs on the walls portraying him offering to Amun-min.

Alexander appointed a Greek banker from Naucratis as Satrap of Egypt in his stead, and from Egypt Alexander went on to his destiny. Less than 10 years later he was dead, but the repercussions of his life meant nothing was quite the same again.

Philip Arrhidaeus

323–317BC

Also known as Meryamun Setepenra. Alexander had lived so intensely and died so young that he left no adult heir. He was succeeded, in name only, by his half-brother Philip Arridaeus, who was a drooling idiot and had been kept shut away; but for now he was the only living male relative of age whose name could be used to hold onto power. No doubt the Macedonian royal family, and especially Alexander's scheming mother, Olympias, were controlling him. But Alexander's empire was too vast to be held by any one ordinary man, let alone a half-wit. Instead, his generals jockeyed for position and poor Philip Arrhidaeus was murdered in 317. On Alexander's death 50 years of struggle saw his empire divided into parts, the Egyptian section falling to Ptolemy, son of Lagus, a childhood friend and, some say, half-brother of Alexander. He had became Satrap of Egypt before Alexander's death after he discovered the corruption of the previous incumbent.Cleomenes, who had stolen, extorted, and robbed temples. Ptolemy sentenced him to death and on Alexander's orders took over.

Alexander IV

317–305BC

Also called Haaibra Setepenamun. Although listed as officially ruling, Alexander IV, Alexander the Great's infant son from his Persian wife Roxanne, had already been murdered along with his mother, and Ptolemy ruled Egypt. He would be followed by his own dynasty.

THE PTOLEMAIC PERIOD 305-30BC

The Ptolemies were products of the Hellenistic age. Though they portrayed themselves as Egyptian and followed the customs of the country, they were essentially Greek in thought and action. Completely a part and product of the modern mediterranean world, their fortunes ebbed and flowed according to their abilities and weaknesses.

Top Right: The colossal sandstone Pylon of the Ptolomaic Temple of Horus at Edfu. On either side of the gateway are statues of the royal Hawk-god. This temple, only cleared fully this century, is the best preserved and most complete in Egypt today. With its walls covered in informative texts that detail its construction history and purpose, it is the brother temple to that dedicated to Hathor at Dendera.

Center Right: A staggering vertical view of the Hypostyle Hall in the Temple of Horus. The ceiling is upheld by 18 columns that recount the protocols of the temple festivals. They retain much of their marvelous paintwork.

Right: Inside the main court of the Temple of Horus, which was built from 237BC to 57BC and replaced an older structure. Through the main gateway the processions arrived, celebrating such festivals as the Feast of the Beautiful Meeting, the annual visit of the goddess Hathor of Dendera to her husband's temple, to celebrate their wedding anniversary.

Ptolemy I

305-282BC

Also known as Soter I and Meryamun Setepenra.

Ptolemy, one of Alexander's most trusted generals, was also probably one of the wisest. Certainly he chose well which segment of his king's great empire he would hold, for unlike the others his portion survived intact for a much longer period. After the death of Alexander, Ptolemy immediately left Babylon and returned to Egypt. Then he waited until Alexander's body passed through nearby Damascus. He kidnapped the body and took it back with him to Memphis, saying that it had been Alexander's wish to be buried at the Shrine of Amun at Siwa. In the end he was buried in Alexandria, the city he founded in the Delta. (The exact location of his tomb remains unknown.) Whether Ptolemy did this through the love of his friend or as a shrewd political

Left: The procession of the Gods on the rear wall of the Temple of Horus at Edfu. Unusually, the temple is oriented to the south, probably because of other structures that are now only evidened, by the merest of archeological traces.

Below Left: A human-headed sphinx from within the temple at Edfu.

Right: View through the monumental gateway erected by Roman emperors Domitian and Trajan towards the Temple of Hathor at Dendera. The gateway opens onto a spacious courtyard containing two birth houses, one from Roman times and the other from the Thirtieth Dynasty. This court and the temple itself were never fully finished, reflecting the political instability of the times.

Below: An elaborately detailed relief panel from the Birth House of Horus at Dendera, dated to the reign of the Roman Emperor Trajan. It shows the emperor as pharaoh, wearing the Red Crown of Lower Egypt and making an offering to Hathor, who is suckling a young Ihy — child of Horus and Hathor — with a second child, also named Ihy, behind.

move is unsure, but it gave him much kudos.

Meanwhile, the generals continued to fight over the spoils of Alexander's vast empire. At times Ptolemy got involved and made alliances, with the result that his empire expanded to encompass Palestine and some of Syria. But it seemed that he was content with what he had — he knew and understood his limitations.

He legitimized his rule in the classic fashion, by marrying a daughter of Nakhthoreb, but he also married Eurydice, the daughter of the Regent of Macedon, by whom he had four children, and Berenice, by whom he had another three. He began what would become one of Egypt's largest building programs, ranging from the development of the new city, Alexandria, soon to be famous for its Pharos and its library, to the restoration of existing temples and the building of new ones.

In 285BC Ptolemy made co-regent his son Ptolemy II from his wife Berenice

Ptolemy II

285-246BC

Also known as Ptolemy Philadelphus and Userkaenra Meryamun.

Ptolemy II co-ruled with his father for about two years before he succeeded him to the throne. His long reign built further on his father's success, increasing Egypt's Mediterranean possessions while increasing internal prosperity and stability. The building work continued and Alexandria flourished.

Ptolemy married Arsinoe, the daughter of Alexander's general Lysimachus, now ruler of Thrace, and had three children by her, but he also married another Arsinoe, his sister, hence his name Philadelphus — "lover of his sister." It was she who adopted her namesake's children following her banishmant for treason.

Above Left: View of the facade of Hathor's Temple at Dendera. Dating from the reign of Tiberius, it is lavishly decorated and its pillars are Hathor-headed.

Left: The sanctuary or Great Seat of the goddess Hathor at Dendera is a free-standing stone chapel whose walls are somewhat battered.

Above Right: A later European representation of Ptolemy II.

Ptolemy III

246-222BC

Also known as Ptolemy Euergetes I and Iwaennetjerwysenwy Sekhemankhra Setepamun.

Son of Arsinoe and Ptolemy II who inherited his father's throne aged around 30. He was married to Berenice, daughter of the king of Cyrenaica. After his sister, married to Antiochus II of Syria, was poisoned in a court conspiracy along with her husband, he sacked Antioch, staying to campaign for a further five years before returning to put down a small rising within Egypt.

His long reign continued to build on those of his two predecessors. The temples continued to rise and the country to prosper. He began the great temple to Horus at Edfu, though it was not to be finished in his reign.

PTOLEMY IV

222-205BC

Also named Iwaennetjerwymenkhwy Setepptah Userkara Sekhemankhamun and Ptolemy IV Philopator.

Eldest son of Ptolemy III and Berenice. He was of a different mold to his forbears, leading a dissolute life of indulgence with the help of various lackeys who encouraged his weaknesses and excesses. As his ineptitude became apparent, Antiochus III of Syria moved in to make a killing. Ptolemy Philopator then briefly stepped out of character, stalled Antiochus with a truce while he raised a mercenary force with which he defeated Antiochus at the battle of Raphia in 217BC. There were then a few minor native uprisings which were soon quelled.

Ptolemy married his sister, Arsinoe, who bore him a son, Ptolemy V. However, he soon took up with another woman, Agathoclea, who with her brother and partner in crime, Agathocles, came to have almost total power over him by pandering to his vices. Ptolemy died — as he had lived — through excess; his wife was almost immediately poisoned off by Agathoclea and Agathocles, who were in their turn discovered and killed.

PTOLEMY V

205–180BC

Also named Ptolemy Epiphanes and Iwaennetjerwymerwyitu Setepptah Userkara Sekhemankhamun.

Ptolemy V was crowned at Memphis, age 12, in an attempt to calm a dangerous situation. Other states, quick to scent any weakness in their rivals, were already picking off Egypt's possessions abroad. Alliances were formed and the monarchy bolstered until Ptolemy V came into his own. In 192BC he married Cleopatra (I), the daughter of Antiochus the Great, by whom he had two sons and a daughter.

PTOLEMY VI

180–164BC and 163–145BC

Also known as Iwaennetjerwyper Setepenptahkhepri Irmaatenamunra and Ptolemy Philomator.

Ptolemy VI was the eldest son of Ptolemy V, and came to the throne early like his father. During his immature years his mother, Cleopatra (I), acted as regent, but on her death two corrupt palace officials saw their opportunity and stepped in. They soon came to grief, when in 170BC, they declared war on Antiochus IV of Syria, who defeated them with ease and captured Ptolemy Philomator.

The Egyptians promptly declared his younger brother, Ptolemy Euergetes, king. Thus there were two Ptolemies, both of whom had been crowned king of Egypt. Both sides now appealed to the latest power emerging in the Mediterranean — Rome. An empire in ascendancy and on the point of taking up the mantle of leadership, Rome was at that time coming to grips with Greek powers all over the eastern Mediterranean. The judgment of Rome led to compromise: Ptolemy Philometor ruled in the old capital of Memphis and Ptolemy Euergetes ruled in the new one of Alexandria.

Matters did not rest here, however, as now both Ptolemies appealed to Rome against Antiochus (who had invaded) and each other. Again Rome passed judgment, confirming Ptolemy VI as King of Egypt and making his younger brother King of Cyrenaica. A Rubicon had been crossed in the future of the Mediterranean powers, though it did not manifest itself immediately.

The remainder of Ptolemy VI's reign was fairly uneventful. He died in combat in Syria, where he had gone to the aid of his daughter Cleopatra I in yet another dynastic dispute.

PTOLEMY VII

145BC

Also known as Ptolemy Neos Philopator.

When his father died in Syria, Ptolemy Neos Philopator was the heir apparent, though in reality too young to rule However his uncle, Ptolemy Euergetes King of Cyrenaica, saw his chance to seize power once again, and took it. Queen Cleopatra and the young heir fled south, but were coaxed back by Euergetes. She eventually agreed to marry Euergetes to safeguard her son's life and enable him to inherit. Her plan backfired when Euergetes poisoned off his nephew.

PTOLEMY VIII

170–163BC and 145–116BC

Also known as Ptolemy Euergetes II.

His despicable deed cleared all obstacles to the throne and the devious Ptolemy VIII Euergetes became king of Egypt. His eye was next caught by his wife's daughter and his niece, another Cleopatra (III). Soon he was married to both of them, but hatred of him grew till he had to flee the country. In his place his sister, Cleopatra II, ruled. But Ptolemy Euergetes was not finished yet; he killed his son by his sister, Memphites, and sent her his body. Then in 129BC he invaded Egypt from Cyprus and took back his throne.

The head of Cleopatra: famed for her beauty, she bore Julius Caesar a son, Caesarion. The Roman general found in her favor in the dispute between her and her brother over the throne of Egypt.

Ptolemy IX

116-110BC, 109-107BC and 88-80BC

Also known as Soter II.

When Ptolemy Euergetes died, his younger wife, Cleopatra III, inherited the throne and ruled as regent in place of one of her sons. She favored the younger Ptolemy X (also known as Alexander I), but by popular demand the elder Ptolemy IX — also known as Ptolemy Soter II — ruled with them. He was then maneuvered out of the frame for a time when he was accused of treason and fled to Cyprus. When his younger brother was chased off the throne he returned, finishing his reign in 80BC.

Ptolemy X

110–109BC and 107–88BC

Also known as Alexander I.

Though favored by his mother, Ptolemy X was not loved by his people. Obese and dissolute, his reckless lifestyle disgusted everyone. It is even suspected he had a hand in his mother's death, despite the fact that with her gone there was no one to support him. He died when he was caught at sea, fleeing westwards.

Ptolemy XI

80BC

Also known as Alexander II.

Ptolemy XI came to the throne through his marriage to Berenice, the daughter of Ptolemy IX. He loathed this older woman, who had brought the throne to him. Thinking to rule alone, he soon had her murdered. When this was discovered an angry mob burst into the palace and lynched him.

Left: Another somewhat Europeanized portrait of Queen Cleopatra, last of the Ptolemaic Dynasty. This famous ruler clung tenaciously to power until she was eclipsed by Roman might.

Right: Female slaves entertaining Ptolemy XIV, younger brother and sometime husband of Queen Cleopatra.

Ptolemy XII

80–58BC and 55–51BC

Also known as Iwaenpanetjernehem Setepptah Irmaat and Neos Dionysos.

To fill a void in the royal dynasty, the illegitimate children of Ptolemy IX and a concubine were brought forward, the eldest of the two boys being crowned Ptolemy XII Neos Dionysos. He was an unpopular monarch who constantly sought the approval of Rome; eventually, he fled there when the people rose against him. When he returned after the short reign of his wilful daughter Berenice, it was Roman power behind him, and he had a brief reign as a shadow king. The writing was on the wall and Rome had come of age.

Queen Berenice IV

58–55BC

When Ptolemy XII was de-throned, only his daughter Berenice was left as heir; she could not rule without a male consort and so married a cousin from the Selucid Syrian dynasty.

The throne achieved, she had her husband assassinated soon after the marriage. She then married an old friend, Archelaus, and they ruled for about four years until Ptolemy XII returned with his mercenary Roman legions to defeat them. Afterwards Berenice was captured and later poisoned.

Queen Cleopatra VII

51–30BC

Also named Netjeret-merites.

This is *the* Cleopatra, mistress of both Mark Anthony and Julius Caesar. The now mythical queen did whatever she could to maintain her country's independence: but it was not to be. Even such a strong woman as Cleopatra could not change the inevitable tide of history.

When Ptolemy XII died, he left his daughter Cleopatra VII the throne, on the condition that she marry her eldest brother Ptolemy XIII. He had other ideas, that included her destruction, but before he could achieve it, Cleopatra had been warned and fled to relatives in Syria.

She was soon back with an army to reclaim her kingdom, though before the showdown could take place, events were taken out of their hands. The Romans, themselves involved in power struggles, burst onto the scene in the form of Pompey and Julius Caesar.

Pompey sought the protection of Ptolemy XIII — in vain: his head was delivered to Caesar, who then sat in judgment on the case between bother and sister. He found in favor of Cleopatra and restored her to the throne. Ptolemy died attacking the Romans.

Cleopatra now married her younger brother, Ptolemy XIV. At the

same time she began an affair with Caesar and bore him a son, Ptolemy XV Caesarion. When Caesar returned to Rome she was secure on her throne: he never saw her again.

Instead, after his murder the Roman Empire was fought over yet again — this time Cleopatra backed the loser, Anthony, paying for this mistake with the loss of her kingdom. Finally out-maneuvered, Cleopatra committed suicide rather than face humiliation at the hands of Rome. When she died Egypt lost a very clever and capable leader and the Ptolemaic Dynasty ended.

Left and This Page: Exterior and interior views of the Ptolemaic Temple at Kom Ombo, unusually dedicated to two gods: Harwer (Horus the Elder) and the crocodile-headed Sobek. Each deity had its own sanctuary and many other features of the temple were doubled as well, including the inner enclosure wall.

THE ROMAN PERIOD

Following the defeat of Anthony and Cleopatra, Egypt lost its sovereignty and became a possession of the new chief Mediterranean power — Rome — though she did not become a province in the normal way. Instead, beginning with Octavian (who became Augustus the first emperor in 27BC), Egypt became a personal estate managed exclusively by and for the first citizen. For a long time the value of the Nile had been recognised for what it was — the bread-basket of the ancient world. Such a resource could not be jeopardized and so the exclusive control of the emperor was justified to the Romans.

The emperors continued to observe the forms of the old religion, commissioning temple restoration and completion, and portraying themselves in the time-honored fashion in the reliefs. In this period of Roman peace, Egypt enjoyed a high standard of stability and prosperity, with new cities expanding along with the agricultural base that had to provide for many more than its indigenous population. Until the adoption of Christianity by Rome, the old gods were still worshipped and, perhaps much more than we credit, survived in the new religious regime.

Above: Julius Caesar.

Below Left: Octavian, later called Augustus.

Below: A Roman Emperor portrayed as an Egyptian pharaoh.

Far left: The Ptolemeic Temple of Harwer at Kom Ombo.

Previous Page, These Pages and Overleaf: Views of the Greco-Roman Isis Temple complex at Philae Island. The site seems to have developed from about the Twenty-Fifth Dynasty as an adjunct to the shrine to Osiris on nearby Biga island.

The earliest visible structure is a kiosk of Nakhtnebef, from the Thirtieth Dynasty. To the north of this lie the ruins of a Ptolemaic temple dedicated to the Nubian deity of Arensnuphis. Between these two is the entrance to the forecourt of the Great Temple of Isis. This forecourt has Roman colonnades to the east and west. There are also chapels dedicated to the Nubian solar-deity Mandulis, and Imhotep, the deified architect of the famous Step Pyramid.

The temple contains parts built by various Ptolemies: the main gateway by Ptolemy II, the towers of the First Pylon by Ptolemy XII, a birth house in the first court by Ptolemy VI, colonnades and the Second Pylon by Ptolemy VIII, and decorations by Ptolemy XII. On the west of the island is a tiny temple dedicated to Hathor built by Ptolemy VI. The Romans added some details too, including a gateway by Hadrian and the famous kiosk of Trajan.

LIST OF PHARAOHS

The complete chronological list of pharaohs is problematic to present accurately: there are areas of doubt, where records either conflict, contradict, or even do not exist at all.

PRE-DYNASTIC PERIOD or Dynasty 0
c.3500-3100BC

SCORPION
NARMER

First Dynasty
3100–2686BC

HOR-AHA
c.3100BC

DJER
c.3000BC

DJET
c.2980BC

DEN
c.2950BC

ANEDJIB
c.2925BC

SEMERKHET
c.2900BC

QA'A
c.2890BC

Second Dynasty
2890–2686BC

HETEPSEKHEMWY
c.2890BC

RANEB
c.2865BC

NYNETJER
c.2825BC

SETH-PERIBSEN
c.2750BC

KHASEKHEMWY
c.2685BC

THE OLD KINGDOM
2686–2181BC

Third Dynasty
2686–2613BC

SANAKHTE
2686-2667BC

DJOSER
2667-2648BC

SEKHEMKHET
2648–2640BC

KHABA
2640–2637BC

HUNI
2637–2613BC

Fourth Dynasty
2613–2494BC

SNEFRU
2613-2589BC

KHUFU
2589-2566BC

DJEDEFRA
2566-2558BC

KHAFRA
2558-2532BC

MENKAURA
2532-2503BC

SHEPSESKAF
2503-2498BC

Fifth Dynasty
2494-2345BC

USERKAF
2494-2487BC

SAHURA
2487-2475BC

NEFERIRKARA
2475-2455BC

Left: A schist statue of pharaoh Menkaura with the goddess Hathor. Though having the smallest pyramid of the Giza field, with a valley temple built of mudbrick rather than stone, more statues of this king have survived than of Khafra or Khufu. Perhaps the legend is true that he was concerned more with the welfare of his people than in expending resources on his monument.

Below: A diorite-gneiss seated statue of Khafra, wearing the *nemes* headcloth, an acknowledged masterpiece of Old Kingdom art. The Sphinx, too, is thought to bear the face of Khafra, carved when the outcrop was incorporated into his funerary complex.

SHEPSESKARA
2455-2448BC

RANEFEREF
2448-2445BC

NYUSERRA
2445-2421BC

MENKAUHOR
2421-2414BC

DJEDKARA
2414-2375BC

UNAS
2375-2345BC

Sixth Dynasty
2345-2181BC

TETI
2345-2323BC

USERKARA
2323-2321BC

PEPI I
2321-2287BC

MERENRA
2287-2278BC

PEPI II
2278-2184BC

THE FIRST INTERMEDIATE PERIOD
2181-2055BC

Seventh & Eighth Dynasties
2181-2125BC

WADJKARE

QUAKARE IBY

Ninth & Tenth Dynasties
2160-2025BC

KHETY I
KHETY II
NEFERKARE
KANEFERRE
KHETY III
KHETY IV
KHETY V

Eleventh Dynasty
2125-2055BC

INTEF I
2125-2112BC

INTEF II
2112-2063BC

INTEF III
2063-2055BC

THE MIDDLE KINGDOM
2055-1650BC

MENTUHOTEP II
2055-2004BC

MENTUHOTEP III
2004-1992BC

MENTUHOTEP IV
1992-1985BC

Twelfth Dynasty
1985-1795BC

AMENEMHAT I
1985-1955BC

SENUSRET I
1965-1920BC

AMENEMHAT II
1922-1878BC

SENUSRET II
1880-1874BC

SENUSRET III
1874-1855BC

AMENEMHAT III
1855-1808BC

AMENEMHET IV
1808-1799BC

QUEEN SOBEKNEFRU
1799-1795BC

Thirteenth Dynasty
1795 to after 1650BC

WEGAF
AMENY INTEF IV
HOR
SOBEKHOTEP III
KHENDJER
SOBEKHOTEP IV
NEFERHOTEP I

Fourteenth Dynasty
1750-1650BC
No names but overlaps with Thirteenth Dynasty.

THE SECOND INTERMEDIATE PERIOD
1650-1550BC

Fifteenth Dynasty
1650-1550BC
Hyksos rulers following successful invasion.

SHESHI
YAKUBHER
KHYAN
APEPI I
APEPI II

Sixteenth Dynasty
1650-1550BC

ANATHER
YAKOBAAM

Left: A statue of Akhenaten's principal queen, Nefertiti. In the Amarna period she seemed to predominate in the wall reliefs and carvings up until the twelfth year of Akhenaten's reign, when she suddenly vanishes. Her remains have never been found, giving rise to the speculation that her body might have been destroyed along with that of her husband.

Far Left: A bust of Thutmose III, wearing the White Crown of Upper Egypt. Another king who had to wait for his inheritance, Thutmose was squeezed out by his mother-in-law Hatshepsut, who delayed his succession for 20 years.

Below Left: Amenhotep III. Father of Akhenaten, he may have had more of a hand in his son's artistic and religious changes than was first realized. In fact, during Amenhotep III's long reign the arts became more naturalistic and it seems he chose the Aten as his personal god, though, unlike his son, he did not insist everyone else should.

Below: Amenhotep IV, otherwise known as the heretical pharaoh Akhenaten. It is now thought that Akhenaten may have suffered from Marfan's disease. Affected individuals grow very tall, their fingers becoming long and spidery, with the chest and spine developing deformities.

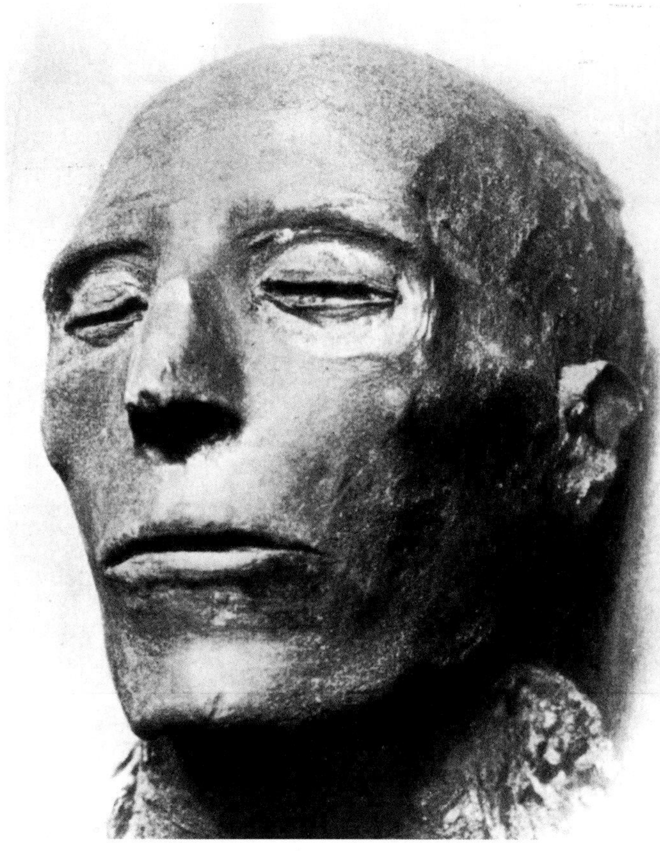

Left: The mummified head of Ramesses II, found in the Great Royal Cache at Deir el-Bahari along with his father Set I and his son and successor Merneptah. All have similar family features.

Below Left: Ramesses III wearing the White Crown of Upper Egypt. He was the last of the truly great pharaohs, who managed to contain the encroaching Mediteranean world, defeating the coalition of Sea Peoples and the Libyans. Though he bore the same name he was not related to either Ramesses I or II.

Seventeenth Dynasty
1650-1550BC

SOBEKEMSAF II
INTEF VII
TAO I
TAO II
KAMOSE

THE NEW KINGDOM
1550-1069BC

Eighteenth Dynasty
1550-1295BC

AHMOSE I
1550-1295BC

AMENHOTEP I
1525-1504BC

THUTMOSE I
1504-1492BC

THUTMOSE II
1492-1479BC

QUEEN HATSHEPSUT
1473-1458BC

TUTHMOSIS III
1479-1425BC

AMENHOTEP II
1427-1400BC

THUTMOSE IV
1400-1390BC

AMENHOTEP III
1390-1352BC

AKHENATEN
1352-1336BC

SMENKHKARA
1338-1336BC

TUTANKHAMUN
1336-1327BC

AY
1327-1323BC

HOREMBEB
1323-1295BC

Nineteenth Dynasty
1295-1186BC

RAMESSES I
1295-1294BC

SETI I
1294-1279BC

RAMESSES II
1279-1213BC

MERNEPTAH
1213-1203BC

AMENMESSES
1203-1200BC

SETI II
1200-1194BC

SIPTAH
1194-1188BC

TWOSRET
11988-1186BC

Twentieth Dynasty
1186-1069BC

SETNAKHTE
1186-1184BC

RAMESSES III
1184-1153BC

RAMESSES IV
1153-1147BC

RAMESSES V
1147-1143BC

RAMESSES VI
1143-1136BC

RAMESSES VII
1136-1129BC

RAMESSES VIII
1129-1126BC

RAMESSES IX
1126-1108BC

RAMESSES X
1108-1099BC

RAMESSES XI
1099-1069BC

THE THIRD INTERMEDIATE PERIOD
1069-525BC
High priest kings in Thebes

HERIHOR
1080-1074BC

PIANKH
1074-1070BC

PINEDJEM I
1070-1032BC

MASAHERTA
1054-1046BC

MENKHEPERRE
1045-992BC

SMENDES II
992-990BC

PINEDJEM II
990-969BC

Right: A portrait of Seti II, from his tomb in the Valley of the Kings. He was the rightful successor of Merneptah, but had to wait five years before he could claim his inheritance because a rival claimant, Amenmesses, usurped the throne. Seti's tomb was not completed and his mummy was found in the smaller Royal Cache inside the tomb of Amenhotep II, where it had been re-interred during the Twenty-First Dynasty.

Below Right: A quartzite seated statue of Seti II, from Thebes, bearing his cartouche on its right shoulder. When he finally came to the throne his reign was very short, lasting no more than six years.

PSUSENNES III
969-945BC

Twenty-first Dynasty
1069-945BC
Based at Tanis on the Delta

SMENDES I
1069-1043BC

AMENEMNISU
1043-1039BC

PSUSENNES I
1039-991BC

AMENEMOPE
993-984BC

OSORKON (the Elder)
984-978BC

SIAMUN
978-959BC

PSUSENNES II
959-945BC

Twenty-second Dynasty
945-715BC
At Bubastis, overlaps with Twenty-third and Twenty-fourth Dynasties

SHESHONQ I
945-924BC

OSORKON I
924-889BC

SHESHONQ II
890BC

TAKELOT I
889-874BC

OSORKON II
874-850BC

TAKELOT II
850-825BC

SHESHONQ III
825-773BC

PAMI
773-767BC

SHESHONQ V
767-730BC

OSORKON IV
730-715BC

Twenty-third Dynasty
818-715BC At Tanis

PEDIBASTET
818-793BC

SHESHONQ IV
793-787BC

OSORKON III
787-759BC

RUDAMON
757-754BC

IUPUT
754-715BC

At Herakleopolis
PEFTJAUABASTET

At Hermopolis
NIMLOT

Twenty-fourth Dynasty
727-715BC At Sais

TEFNAKHT
727-720BC

BAKENRENEF
727-715BC

Twenty-fifth Dynasty
747-656BC
Kushite rulers, overlap with Twenty-sixth Dynasty

PIANKHI
747-716BC

SHABAKA
716-702BC

SHEBITKU
702-690BC

TAHARQA
690-664BC

TANUTAMUN
664-656BC

Twenty-sixth Dynasty
664-525BC

PSAMTIK I
664-610BC

NEKAU
610-595BC

PSAMTIK II
595-589BC

WAHIBRA
589-570BC

AHMOSE II
570-526BC

PSAMTIK III
526-525BC

FIRST PERSIAN PERIOD

Twenty-seventh Dynasty
525-404BC

CAMBYSES II
525-522BC

DARIUS I
521-486BC

XERXES
485-465BC

ARTAXERXES I
464-424BC

DARIUS II
423-405BC

ARTAXERXES II
405-359BC

Twenty-eighth Dynasty
404-399BC

AMYRTAEUS
404-399BC

Twenty-ninth Dynasty
399-380BC

NEFAARUD I
399-393BC

HAKOR
393-380BC

Thirtieth Dynasty
380-343BC

NAKHTNEBEF
380-362BC

DJEDHOR
362-360BC

NAKHTHOREB
or Nectanebo
360-343BC

Nectanebo (Greek name) is considered to be the last indigenous pharaoh, the ruling position taken thereafter by either the governor appointed by, or the emperor of, the ruling power.

SECOND PERSIAN PERIOD
343-332BC

ARTAXERXES III
343-338BC

ARSES
338-336BC

DARIUS III
336-332BC

MACEDONIAN PERIOD
332-305BC

ALEXANDER THE GREAT
332-323BC

PHILIP ARRHIDAEUS
323-317BC

ALEXANDER IV
317-305BC

PTOLEMAIC PERIOD
305-30BC

PTOLEMY I
305-282BC

PTOLEMY II
285-246BC

PTOLEMY III
246-222BC

PTOLEMY IV
222-205BC

PTOLEMY V
205-180BC

PTOLEMY VI
180-164 and 163-145BC

PTOLEMY VII
145BC

PTOLEMY VIII
170-163 and 145-116BC

PTOLEMY IX
116-110, 109-107 and 88-80BC

PTOLEMY X
110-109 and 107-88BC

PTOLEMY XI
80BC

PTOLEMY XII
80-58BC and 55-51BC

QUEEN BERENICE IV
58-55BC

QUEEN CLEOPATRA VII
51-30BC

ROMAN PERIOD

Until the division of the Empire in 394 AD, Egypt was ruled as a Roman province. The emperors were venerated as pharaohs.

AUGUSTUS
30BC-AD14

TIBERIUS
AD14-37

GAIUS (CALIGULA)
37-41

CLAUDIUS
41-54

NERO
54-68

GALBA
68-69

OTHO
69

VESPASIAN
69-79

TITUS
79-81

DOMITIAN
81-96

NERVA
96-98

TRAJAN
98-117

HADRIAN
117-138

ANTONINUS PIUS
138-161

MARCUS AURELIUS
161-169

LUCIUS VERUS
169-180

COMMODUS
180-192

SEPTIMUS SEVERUS
193-211

GETA
211

CARACALLA
211-217

MACRINUS
217-218

DIDUMENIAN
218

ELAGABALUS
218-222

SEVERUS ALEXANDER
222-235

MAXIMUS
235-238

GORD IAN I
238

GORDIAN II
238

GORDIAN III
238-244

PHILIP I
244-249

PHILIP II
247-249

DECIUS
249-251

GALLUS
251-253

VALERIAN
253-260

GALLIENUS
253-268

MACRIANUS
268-270

AURELIAN
270-275

PROBUS
276-282

CARUS
282-283

NUMERIAN
283-284

CARINUS
284-285

DIOCLETIAN
284-305

MAXIMIAN
286-305

CONSTANTIUS I
305-306

GALERIUS
305-311

MAXENTIUS
307-312

CONSTANTINE I
307-337

LICINIUS
308-324

MAXIMENUS DAIA
310-313

CONSTANTINE I
337-340

CONSTANS
337-350

CONSTANTIUS II
337-361

MAGNETIUS
350-353

JULIAN THE APOSTATE
360-363

JOVIAN
363-364

VELENTINIAN I
364-375

VALENS
364-378

GRATIAN
375-383

VALENTINIAN II
375-392

THEODOSIUS
379-395

EUGENIUS
392-394

INDEX

PHOTO CREDITS

The Publisher is grateful to the following for their kind permission to reproduce the photographs on these pages:

A.N.T. Photo Library: 9, 10, 11, 13, 14, 16/7, 18 (both), 20, 22 (T), 23, 24, 25, 27, 28, 30, 32, 33 (T), 39, 45, 46, 47 (both), 52 (B), 54/5, 59, 67, 68/9, 71 (T), 74/5, 76, 77, 78, 83, 86 (T), 88 (T), 90, 96 (T), 101, 102 (both), 105(B), 106 (both), 119 (all three), 120 (B), 121 (B), 122 (both), 129 (both), 130, 131 (BR), 132/3, 134 (all three), 135 (T).

Archive Photos: 21, 31 (T), 63, 73, 81 (R), 84, 91 (both), 98, 111, 112, 116, 117, 118, 123, 125, 126, 127, 131 (BL and T).

BPL: 25 (B), 26, 29 (B), 31 (B), 33 (B), 40/1, 43, 68 (T), 87 (B), 88 (B), 89, 94 (T), 95 (B), 97.

Christie's Images, London: 12, 19, 30, 61, 64, 65, 80, 81 (L).

Hulton Getty: 136, 137, 138, 139 (all three), 140 (both), 141 (both).

Image Bank: 15, 29 (T), 86 (T), 93, 94 (B), 95 (T), 96 (B), 103, 104, 105 (T).

Ian Sidaway: 8, 35, 36/7, 48/9, 50/1 (both), 52 (T), 52/3, 70/1, 85, 109, 114/5, 120 (T), 121 (T), 128 (both), 135 (B).